LaTeX2e: An unofficial reference manual

August 2017

http://puszcza.gnu.org.ua/software/latexrefman/

This document is an unofficial reference manual for LaTeX, a document preparation system, version of August 2017.

This manual was originally translated from `LATEX.HLP` v1.0a in the VMS Help Library. The pre-translation version was written by George D. Greenwade of Sam Houston State University. The LaTeX 2.09 version was written by Stephen Gilmore. The LaTeX2e version was adapted from this by Torsten Martinsen. Karl Berry made further updates and additions, and gratefully acknowledges using *Hypertext Help with LaTeX*, by Sheldon Green, and *LaTeX Command Summary* (for LaTeX 2.09) by L. Botway and C. Biemesderfer (published by the TeX Users Group as *TeXniques* number 10), as reference material (no text was directly copied).

Short Contents

Table of Contents

LaTeX2e: An unofficial reference manual

This document is an unofficial reference manual (version of August 2017) for LaTeX2e, a document preparation system.

1 About this document

This is an unofficial reference manual for the LaTeX2e document preparation system, which is a macro package for the TeX typesetting program (see Chapter 2 [Overview], page 3). This document's home page is `http://puszcza.gnu.org.ua/software/latexrefman/`. That page has links to the current output in various formats, sources, mailing list archives and subscriptions, and other infrastructure.

In this document, we will mostly just use 'LaTeX' rather than 'LaTeX2e', since the previous version of LaTeX (2.09) was frozen decades ago.

LaTeX is currently maintained by a group of volunteers (`http://latex-project.org`). The official documentation written by the LaTeX project is available from their web site. This document is completely unofficial and has not been reviewed by the LaTeX maintainers. Do not send bug reports or anything else about this document to them. Instead, please send all comments to `latexrefman@tug.org`.

This document is a reference. There is a vast array of other sources of information about LaTeX, at all levels. Here are a few introductions.

`http://ctan.org/pkg/latex-doc-ptr`
>   Two pages of recommended references to LaTeX documentation.

`http://ctan.org/pkg/first-latex-doc`
>   Writing your first document, with a bit of both text and math.

`http://ctan.org/pkg/usrguide`
>   The guide for document authors that is maintained as part of LaTeX. Many other guides by many other people are also available, independent of LaTeX itself; one such is the next item:

`http://ctan.org/pkg/lshort`
>   A short introduction to LaTeX, translated to many languages.

`http://tug.org/begin.html`
>   Introduction to the TeX system, including LaTeX, with further references.

2 Overview of LaTeX

LaTeX is a system for typesetting documents. It was originally created by Leslie Lamport and is now maintained by a group of volunteers (http://latex-project.org). It is widely used, particularly for complex and technical documents, such as those involving mathematics.

A LaTeX user writes an input file containing text along with interspersed commands, for instance commands describing how the text should be formatted. It is implemented as a set of related commands that interface with Donald E. Knuth's TeX typesetting program (the technical term is that LaTeX is a *macro package* for the TeX engine). The user produces the output document by giving that input file to the TeX engine.

The term LaTeX is also sometimes used to mean the language in which the document is marked up, that is, to mean the set of commands available to a LaTeX user.

The name LaTeX is short for "Lamport TeX". It is pronounced LAH-teck or LAY-teck, or sometimes LAY-tecks. Inside a document, produce the logo with `\LaTeX`. Where use of the logo is not sensible, such as in plain text, write it as 'LaTeX'.

2.1 Starting and ending

LaTeX files have a simple global structure, with a standard beginning and ending. Here is a "hello, world" example:

```
\documentclass{article}
\begin{document}
Hello, \LaTeX\ world.
\end{document}
```

Here, the 'article' is the so-called *document class*, implemented in a file `article.cls`. Any document class can be used. A few document classes are defined by LaTeX itself, and vast array of others are widely available. See Chapter 3 [Document classes], page 8.

You can include other LaTeX commands between the `\documentclass` and the `\begin{document}` commands. This area is called the *preamble*.

The `\begin{document}` ... `\end{document}` is a so-called *environment*; the 'document' environment (and no others) is required in all LaTeX documents (see Section 8.6 [document], page 41). LaTeX provides many environments itself, and many more are defined separately. See Chapter 8 [Environments], page 37.

The following sections discuss how to produce PDF or other output from a LaTeX input file.

2.2 Output files

LaTeX produces a main output file and at least two accessory files. The main output file's name ends in either `.dvi` or `.pdf`.

`.dvi`   If LaTeX is invoked with the system command `latex` then it produces a DeVice Independent file, with extension `.dvi`. You can view this file with a command such as `xdvi`, or convert it to a PostScript `.ps` file with `dvips` or to a Portable Document Format `.pdf` file with `dvipdfmx`. The contents of the file can be

.pdf   dumped in human-readable form with `dvitype`. A vast array of other DVI utility programs are available (http://mirror.ctan.org/dviware).

.pdf   If LaTeX is invoked via the system command `pdflatex`, among other commands (see Section 2.3 [TeX engines], page 4), then the main output is a Portable Document Format (PDF) file. Typically this is a self-contained file, with all fonts and images included.

LaTeX also produces at least two additional files.

.log   This transcript file contains summary information such as a list of loaded packages. It also includes diagnostic messages and perhaps additional information for any errors.

.aux   Auxiliary information is used by LaTeX for things such as cross references. For example, the first time that LaTeX finds a forward reference—a cross reference to something that has not yet appeared in the source—it will appear in the output as a doubled question mark `??`. When the referred-to spot does eventually appear in the source then LaTeX writes its location information to this `.aux` file. On the next invocation, LaTeX reads the location information from this file and uses it to resolve the reference, replacing the double question mark with the remembered location.

LaTeX may produce yet more files, characterized by the filename ending. These include a `.lof` file that is used to make a list of figures, a `.lot` file used to make a list of tables, and a `.toc` file used to make a table of contents. A particular class may create others; the list is open-ended.

2.3 TeX engines

LaTeX is defined to be a set of commands that are run by a TeX implementation (see Chapter 2 [Overview], page 3). This section gives a terse overview of the main programs.

latex
pdflatex In TeX Live (http://tug.org/texlive), if LaTeX is invoked via either the system command `latex` or `pdflatex`, then the pdfTeX engine is run (http://ctan.org/pkg/pdftex). When invoked as `latex`, the main output is a `.dvi` file; as `pdflatex`, the main output is a `.pdf` file.

pdfTeX incorporates the e-TeX extensions to Knuth's original program (http://ctan.org/pkg/etex), including additional programming features and bi-directional typesetting, and has plenty of extensions of its own. e-TeX is available on its own as the system command `etex`, but this is plain TeX (and produces `.dvi`).

In other TeX distributions, `latex` may invoke e-TeX rather than pdfTeX. In any case, the e-TeX extensions can be assumed to be available in LaTeX.

lualatex If LaTeX is invoked via the system command `lualatex`, the LuaTeX engine is run (http://ctan.org/pkg/luatex). This program allows code written in the scripting language Lua (http://luatex.org) to interact with TeX's typesetting. LuaTeX handles UTF-8 Unicode input natively, can handle OpenType and TrueType fonts, and produces a `.pdf` file by default. There is also `dvilualatex` to produce a `.dvi` file, but this is rarely used.

xelatex   If LaTeX is invoked with the system command `xelatex`, the XeTeX engine is
           run (`http://tug.org/xetex`). Like LuaTeX, XeTeX natively supports UTF-
           8 Unicode and TrueType and OpenType fonts, though the implementation is
           completely different, mainly using external libraries instead of internal code.
           XeTeX produces a `.pdf` file as output; it does not support DVI output.

           Internally, XeTeX creates an `.xdv` file, a variant of DVI, and translates that to
           PDF using the `(x)dvipdfmx` program, but this process is automatic. The `.xdv`
           file is only useful for debugging.

Other variants of LaTeX and TeX exist, e.g., to provide additional support for Japanese
and other languages ([u]pTeX, `http://ctan.org/pkg/ptex`, `http://ctan.org/pkg/uptex`).

2.4 LaTeX command syntax

In the LaTeX input file, a command name starts with a backslash character, \. The name
itself then consists of either (a) a string of letters or (b) a single non-letter.

LaTeX commands names are case sensitive so that `\pagebreak` differs from `\Pagebreak`
(the latter is not a standard command). Most commands are lowercase, but in any event
you must enter all commands in the same case as they are defined.

A command may be followed by zero, one, or more arguments. These arguments may
be either required or optional. Required arguments are contained in curly braces, `{...}`.
Optional arguments are contained in square brackets, `[...]`. Generally, but not universally,
if the command accepts an optional argument, it comes first, before any required arguments.

Inside of an optional argument, to use the character close square bracket (`]`) hide it inside
curly braces, as in `\item[closing bracket {]}]`. Similarly, if an optional argument comes
last, with no required argument after it, then to make the first character of the following
text be an open square bracket, hide it inside curly braces.

LaTeX has the convention that some commands have a * form that is related to the form
without a *, such as `\chapter` and `\chapter*`. The exact difference in behavior varies from
command to command.

This manual describes all accepted options and *-forms for the commands it covers
(barring unintentional omissions, a.k.a. bugs).

2.4.1 Environments

Synopsis:

```
\begin{environment name}
  ...
\end{environment name}
```

An area of LaTeX source, inside of which there is a distinct behavior. For instance, for
poetry in LaTeX put the lines between `\begin{verse}` and `\end{verse}`.

```
\begin{verse}
  There once was a man from Nantucket \\
  ...
\end{verse}
```

See Chapter 8 [Environments], page 37, for a list of environments.

The *environment name* at the beginning must exactly match that at the end. This includes the case where *environment name* ends in a star (*); both the `\begin` and `\end` texts must include the star.

Environments may have arguments, including optional arguments. This example produces a table. The first argument is optional (and causes the table to be aligned on its top row) while the second argument is required (it specifies the formatting of columns).

```
\begin{tabular}[t]{r|l}
  ... rows of table ...
\end{tabular}
```

2.4.2 Command declarations

A command that changes the value, or changes the meaning, of some other command or parameter. For instance, the `\mainmatter` command changes the setting of page numbers from roman numerals to arabic.

2.4.3 `\makeatletter` and `\makeatother`

Synopsis:

```
\makeatletter
  ... definition of commands with @ in their name ..
\makeatother
```

Used to redefine internal LaTeX commands. `\makeatletter` makes the at-sign character @ have the category code of a letter, 11. `\makeatother` sets the category code of @ to 12, its original value.

As each character is read by TeX for LaTeX, it is assigned a character category code, or *catcode* for short. For instance, the backslash \ is assigned the catcode 0, for characters that start a command. These two commands alter the catcode assigned to @.

The alteration is needed because many of LaTeX's commands use @ in their name, to prevent users from accidentally defining a command that replaces one of LaTeX's own. Command names consist of a category 0 character, ordinarily backslash, followed by letters, category 11 characters (except that a command name can also consist of a category 0 character followed by a single non-letter symbol). So under the default category codes, user-defined commands cannot contain an @. But `\makeatletter` and `\makeatother` allow users to define or redefine commands named with @.

Use these two commands inside a `.tex` file, in the preamble, when defining or redefining a command with @ in its name. Don't use them inside `.sty` or `.cls` files since the `\usepackage` and `\documentclass` commands set the at sign to have the character code of a letter.

For a comprehensive list of macros with an at-sign in their names see `http://ctan.org/pkg/macros2e`. These macros are mainly intended to package or class authors.

The example below is typical. In the user's class file is a command `\thesis@universityname`. The user wants to change the definition. These three lines should go in the preamble, before the `\begin{document}`.

```
\makeatletter
\renewcommand{\thesis@universityname}{Saint Michael's College}
\makeatother
```

2.4.3.1 \@ifstar

Synopsis:

```
\newcommand{\mycmd}{\@ifstar{\mycmd@star}{\mycmd@nostar}}
\newcommand{\mycmd@nostar}[non-starred command number of args]{body of non-
starred command}
\newcommand{\mycmd@star}[starred command number of args]{body of starred command}
```

Many standard LaTeX environments or commands have a variant with the same name but ending with a star character *, an asterisk. Examples are the `table` and `table*` environments and the `\section` and `\section*` commands.

When defining environments, following this pattern is straightforward because `\newenvironment` and `\renewenvironment` allow the environment name to contain a star. For commands the situation is more complex. As in the synopsis above, there will be a user-called command, given above as `\mycmd`, which peeks ahead to see if it is followed by a star. For instance, LaTeX does not really have a `\section*` command; instead, the `\section` command peeks ahead. This command does not accept arguments but instead expands to one of two commands that do accept arguments. In the synopsis these two are `\mycmd@nostar` and `\mycmd@star`. They could take the same number of arguments or a different number, or no arguments at all. As always, in a LaTeX document a command using at-sign @ must be enclosed inside a `\makeatletter` ... `\makeatother` block (see Section 2.4.3 [\makeatletter and \makeatother], page 6).

This example of `\@ifstar` defines the command `\ciel` and a variant `\ciel*`. Both have one required argument. A call to `\ciel{night}` will return "starry night sky" while `\ciel*{blue}` will return "starry not blue sky".

```
\newcommand*{\ciel@unstarred}[1]{starry #1 sky}
\newcommand*{\ciel@starred}[1]{starry not #1 sky}
\newcommand*{\ciel}{\@ifstar{\ciel@starred}{\ciel@unstarred}}
```

In the next example, the starred variant takes a different number of arguments than does the unstarred one. With this definition, Agent 007's ``My name is \agentsecret*{Bond}, \agentsecret{James}{Bond}.'' is equivalent to ``My name is \textsc{Bond}, \textit{James} textsc{Bond}.''

```
\newcommand*{\agentsecret@unstarred}[2]{\textit{#1} \textsc{#2}}
\newcommand*{\agentsecret@starred}[1]{\textsc{#1}}
\newcommand*{\agentsecret}{\@ifstar{\agentsecret@starred}{\agentsecret@unstarred}}
```

There are two sometimes more convenient ways to accomplish the work of `\@ifstar`. The `suffix` package allows the construct `\newcommand\mycommand{unstarred version}` followed by `\WithSuffix\newcommand\mycommand*{starred version}`. And LaTeX3 has the `xparse` package that allows this code.

```
\NewDocumentCommand\foo{s}{\IfBooleanTF#1
  {starred version}%
  {unstarred version}%
  }
```

3 Document classes

The document's overall class is defined with this command, which is normally the first command in a LaTeX source file.

> \documentclass[*options*]{*class*}

The following document *class* names are built into LaTeX. (Many other document classes are available as separate packages; see Chapter 2 [Overview], page 3.)

article   For a journal article, a presentation, and miscellaneous general use.

book   Full-length books, including chapters and possibly including front matter, such as a preface, and back matter, such as an appendix (see Chapter 23 [Front/back matter], page 122).

letter   Mail, optionally including mailing labels (see Chapter 24 [Letters], page 124).

report   For documents of length between an article and a book, such as technical reports or theses, which may contain several chapters.

slides   For slide presentations—rarely used today. In its place the beamer package is perhaps the most prevalent (see Section A.1 [beamer template], page 130).

Standard *options* are described in the next section.

3.1 Document class options

You can specify so-called *global options* or *class options* to the \documentclass command by enclosing them in square brackets. To specify more than one *option*, separate them with a comma, as in:

> \documentclass[*option1,option2,...*]{*class*}

Here is the list of the standard class options.

All of the standard classes except slides accept the following options for selecting the typeface size (default is 10pt):

> 10pt   11pt   12pt

All of the standard classes accept these options for selecting the paper size (these show height by width):

a4paper   210 by 297 mm (about 8.25 by 11.75 inches)

a5paper   148 by 210 mm (about 5.8 by 8.3 inches)

b5paper   176 by 250 mm (about 6.9 by 9.8 inches)

executivepaper
            7.25 by 10.5 inches

legalpaper
            8.5 by 14 inches

letterpaper
            8.5 by 11 inches (the default)

When using one of the engines pdfLaTeX, LuaLaTeX, or XeLaTeX (see Section 2.3 [TeX engines], page 4), options other than `letterpaper` set the print area but you must also set the physical paper size. One way to do that is to put `\pdfpagewidth=\paperwidth` and `\pdfpageheight=\paperheight` in your document's preamble. The `geometry` package provides flexible ways of setting the print area and physical page size.

Miscellaneous other options:

`draft`
`final`   Mark (`draft`) or do not mark (`final`) overfull boxes with a black box in the margin; default is `final`.

`fleqn`   Put displayed formulas flush left; default is centered.

`landscape`
                  Selects landscape format; default is portrait.

`leqno`   Put equation numbers on the left side of equations; default is the right side.

`openbib`   Use "open" bibliography format.

`titlepage`
`notitlepage`
                  Specifies whether there is a separate page for the title information and for the abstract also, if there is one. The default for the `report` class is `titlepage`, for the other classes it is `notitlepage`.

The following options are not available with the `slides` class.

`onecolumn`
`twocolumn`
                  Typeset in one or two columns; default is `onecolumn`.

`oneside`
`twoside`   Selects one- or two-sided layout; default is `oneside`, except that in the `book` class the default is `twoside`.

                  For one-sided printing, the text is centered on the page. For two-sided printing, the `\evensidemargin` (`\oddsidemargin`) parameter determines the distance on even (odd) numbered pages between the left side of the page and the text's left margin, with `\oddsidemargin` being 40% of the difference between `\paperwidth` and `\textwidth`, and `\evensidemargin` is the remainder.

`openright`
`openany`   Determines if a chapter should start on a right-hand page; default is `openright` for `book`, and `openany` for `report`.

The `slides` class offers the option `clock` for printing the time at the bottom of each note.

3.2 Additional packages

Load a package *pkg*, with the package options given in the comma-separated list *options*, as here.

        `\usepackage[options]{pkg}`.

To specify more than one package you can separate them with a comma, as in \usepackage{*pkg1*,*pkg2*,...}, or use multiple \usepackage commands.

Any options given in the \documentclass command that are unknown to the selected document class are passed on to the packages loaded with \usepackage.

3.3 Class and package construction

You can create new document classes and new packages. For instance, if your memos must satisfy some local requirements, such as a standard header for each page, then you could create a new class smcmemo.cls and begin your documents with \documentclass{smcmemo}.

What separates a package from a document class is that the commands in a package are useful across classes while those in a document class are specific to that class. Thus, a command to set page headers is for a package while a command to make the page headers say Memo from the SMC Math Department is for a class.

Inside of a class or package file you can use the at-sign @ as a character in command names without having to surround the code containing that command with \makeatletter and \makeatother. See Section 2.4.3 [\makeatletter and \makeatother], page 6. This allow you to create commands that users will not accidentally redefine. Another technique is to preface class- or package-specific commands with some string to prevent your class or package from interfering with others. For instance, the class smcmemo might have commands \smc@tolist, \smc@fromlist, etc.

3.3.1 Class and package structure

A class file or package file typically has four parts.

> In the *identification part*, the file says that it is a LaTeX package or class and describes itself, using the \NeedsTeXFormat and \ProvidesClass or \ProvidesPackage commands.

1. The *preliminary declarations part* declares some commands and can also load other files. Usually these commands will be those needed for the code used in the next part. For example, an smcmemo class might be called with an option to read in a file with a list of people for the to-head, as \documentclass[mathto]{smcmemo}, and therefore needs to define a command \newcommand{\setto}[1]{\def\@tolist{#1}} used in that file.

2. In the *handle options part* the class or package declares and processes its options. Class options allow a user to start their document as \documentclass[*option list*]{*class name*}, to modify the behavior of the class. An example is when you declare \documentclass[11pt]{article} to set the default document font size.

3. Finally, in the *more declarations part* the class or package usually does most of its work: declaring new variables, commands and fonts, and loading other files.

Here is a starting class file, which should be saved as stub.cls where LaTeX can find it, for example in the same directory as the .tex file.

```
\NeedsTeXFormat{LaTeX2e}
\ProvidesClass{stub}[2017/07/06 stub to start building classes from]
\DeclareOption*{\PassOptionsToClass{\CurrentOption}{article}}
\ProcessOptions\relax
\LoadClass{article}
```

It identifies itself, handles the class options via the default of passing them all to the `article` class, and then loads the `article` class to provide the basis for this class's code.

For more, see the official guide for class and package writers, the Class Guide, at `http://www.latex-project.org/help/documentation/clsguide.pdf` (much of the descriptions here derive from this document), or the tutorial `https://www.tug.org/TUGboat/tb26-3/tb84heff.pdf`.

3.3.2 Class and package commands

These are the commands designed to help writers of classes or packages.

`\AtBeginDvi{specials}`

> Save in a box register things that are written to the `.dvi` file at the beginning of the shipout of the first page of the document.

`\AtEndOfClass{code}`
`\AtEndOfPackage{code}`

> Hook to insert *code* to be executed when LaTeX finishes processing the current class or package. You can use these hooks multiple times; the `code` will be executed in the order that you called it. See also ⟨undefined⟩ [\AtBeginDocument], page ⟨undefined⟩.

`\CheckCommand{cmd}[num][default]{definition}`
`\CheckCommand*{cmd}[num][default]{definition}`

> Like `\newcommand` (see Section 12.1 [\newcommand & \renewcommand], page 72) but does not define *cmd*; instead it checks that the current definition of *cmd* is exactly as given by *definition* and is or is not *long* as expected. A long command is a command that accepts `\par` within an argument. The *cmd* command is expected to be long with the unstarred version of `\CheckCommand`. Raises an error when the check fails. This allows you to check before you start redefining `cmd` yourself that no other package has already redefined this command.

`\ClassError{class name}{error text}{help text}`
`\PackageError{package name}{error text}{help text}`
`\ClassWarning{class name}{warning text}`
`\PackageWarning{package name}{warning text}`
`\ClassWarningNoLine{class name}{warning text}`
`\PackageWarningNoLine{package name}{warning text}`
`\ClassInfo{class name}{info text}`
`\PackageInfo{package name}{info text}`
`\ClassInfoNoLine{class name}{info text}`
`\PackageInfoNoLine{package name}{info text}`

> Produce an error message, or warning or informational messages.

> For `\ClassError` and `\PackageError` the message is *error text*, followed by TeX's ? error prompt. If the user then asks for help by typing `h`, they see the *help text*.

> The four warning commands are similar except that they write *warning text* on the screen with no error prompt. The four info commands write *info text*

only in the transcript file. The `NoLine` versions do not show the number of the line generating the message, while the other versions do show that number.

To format the messages, including the *help text*: use `\protect` to stop a command from expanding, get a line break with `\MessageBreak`, and get a space with `\space` when a space character does not allow it, like after a command. Note that LaTeX appends a period to the messages.

`\CurrentOption`

> Expands to the name of the currently-being-processed option. Can only be used within the *code* argument of either `\DeclareOption` or `\DeclareOption*`.

`\DeclareOption{option}{code}`
`\DeclareOption*{code}`

> Make an option available to a user, for invoking in their `\documentclass` command. For example, the `smcmemo` class could have an option allowing users to put the institutional logo on the first page with `\documentclass[logo]{smcmemo}`. The class file must contain `\DeclareOption{logo}{code}` (and later, `\ProcessOptions`).
>
> If you request an option that has not been declared, by default this will produce a warning like `Unused global option(s): [badoption]`. Change this behaviour with the starred version `\DeclareOption*{code}`. For example, many classes extend an existing class, using a declaration such as `\LoadClass{article}`, and for passing extra options to the underlying class use code such as this.

```
\DeclareOption*{%
\PassOptionsToClass{\CurrentOption}{article}%
}
```

> Another example is that the class `smcmemo` may allow users to keep lists of memo recipients in external files. Then the user could invoke `\documentclass[math]{smcmemo}` and it will read the file `math.memo`. This code handles the file if it exists and otherwise passes the option to the `article` class.

```
\DeclareOption*{\InputIfFileExists{\CurrentOption.memo}{}{%
\PassOptionsToClass{\CurrentOption}{article}}}
```

`\DeclareRobustCommand{cmd}[num][default]{definition}`
`\DeclareRobustCommand*{cmd}[num][default]{definition}`

> Like `\newcommand` and `\newcommand*` (see Section 12.1 [\newcommand & \renewcommand], page 72) but these declare a robust command, even if some code within the *definition* is fragile. (For a discussion of robust and fragile commands see Section 12.9 [\protect], page 78.) Use this command to define new robust commands or to redefine existing commands and make them robust. Unlike `\newcommand` these do not give an error if macro *cmd* already exists; instead, a log message is put into the transcript file if a command is redefined.
>
> Commands defined this way are a bit less efficient than those defined using `\newcommand` so unless the command's data is fragile and the command is used within a moving argument, use `\newcommand`.

The `etoolbox` package offers commands `\newrobustcmd`, `\newrobustcmd*`, `\renewrobustcmd`, `\renewrobustcmd*`, `\providerobustcmd`, and `\providerobustcmd*` which are similar to `\newcommand`, `\newcommand*`, `\renewcommand`, `\renewcommand*`, `\providecommand`, and `\providecommand*`, but define a robust *cmd* with two advantages as compared to `\DeclareRobustCommand`:

1. They use the low-level e-TeX protection mechanism rather than the higher level LaTeX `\protect` mechanism, so they do not incur the slight loss of performance mentioned above, and

2. They make the same distinction between `\new...`, `\renew...`, and `\provide...`, as the standard commands, so they do not just make a log message when you redefine *cmd* that already exists, in that case you need to use either `\renew...` or `\provide...` or you get an error.

`\IfFileExists{`*file name*`}{`*true code*`}{`*false code*`}`
`\InputIfFileExists{`*file name*`}{`*true code*`}{`*false code*`}`

Execute *true code* if LaTeX can find the file `file name` and *false code* otherwise. In the second case it inputs the file immediately after executing *true code*. Thus `\IfFileExists{img.pdf}{\includegraphics{img.pdf}}{\typeout{WARNING:` `img.pdf not found}}` will include the graphic `img.pdf` if it is found but otherwise just give a warning.

This command looks for the file in all search paths that LaTeX uses, not only in the current directory. To look only in the current directory do something like `\IfFileExists{./filename}{`*true code*`}{`*false code*`}`. If you ask for a filename without a `.tex` extension then LaTeX will first look for the file by appending the `.tex`; for more on how LaTeX handles file extensions see Section 22.3 [\input], page 121.

`\LoadClass[`*options list*`]{`*class name*`}[`*release date*`]`
`\LoadClassWithOptions{`*class name*`}[`*release date*`]`

Load a class, as with `\documentclass[`*options list*`]{`*class name*`}[`*release info*`]`. An example is `\LoadClass[twoside]{article}`.

The *options list*, if present, is a comma-separated list. The *release date* is optional. If present it must have the form *YYYY/MM/DD*.

If you request a *release date* and the date of the package installed on your system is earlier, then you get a warning on the screen and in the log like `You have requested, on input line 4, version '2038/01/19' of document class article, but only version '2014/09/29 v1.4h Standard LaTeX document class' is available.`

The command version `\LoadClassWithOptions` uses the list of options for the current class. This means it ignores any options passed to it via `\PassOptionsToClass`. This is a convenience command that lets you build classes on existing ones, such as the standard **article** class, without having to track which options were passed.

`\ExecuteOptions{`*options-list*`}`

> For each option *option* in the *options-list*, in order, this command executes the command `\ds@`*option*. If this command is not defined then that option is silently ignored.
>
> It can be used to provide a default option list before `\ProcessOptions`. For example, if in a class file you want the default to be 11pt fonts then you could specify `\ExecuteOptions{11pt}\ProcessOptions\relax`.

`\NeedsTeXFormat{`*format*`}[`*format date*`]`

> Specifies the format that this class must be run under. Often issued as the first line of a class file, and most often used as: `\NeedsTeXFormat{LaTeX2e}`. When a document using that class is processed, the format name given here must match the format that is actually being run (including that the *format* string is case sensitive). If it does not match then execution stops with an error like 'This file needs format 'LaTeX2e' but this is 'xxx'.'
>
> To specify a version of the format that you know to have certain features, include the optional *format date* on which those features were implemented. If present it must be in the form `YYYY/MM/DD`. If the format version installed on your system is earlier than *format date* then you get a warning like 'You have requested release '2038/01/20' of LaTeX, but only release '2016/02/01' is available.'

`\OptionNotUsed`

> Adds the current option to the list of unused options. Can only be used within the *code* argument of either `\DeclareOption` or `\DeclareOption*`.

`\PassOptionsToClass{`*option list*`}{`*class name*`}`
`\PassOptionsToPackage{`*option list*`}{`*package name*`}`

> Adds the options in the comma-separated list *option list* to the options used by any future `\RequirePackage` or `\usepackage` command for package *package name* or the class *class name*.
>
> The reason for these commands is: you may load a package any number of times with no options but if you want options then you may only supply them when you first load the package. Loading a package with options more than once will get you an error like `Option clash for package foo`. (LaTeX throws an error even if there is no conflict between the options.)
>
> If your own code is bringing in a package twice then you can collapse that to once, for example replacing the two `\RequirePackage[landscape]{geometry}\Requir` with the single `\RequirePackage[landscape,margins=1in]{geometry}`. But if you are loading a package that in turn loads another package then you need to queue up the options you desire for this other package. For instance, suppose the package `foo` loads the package `geometry`. Instead of `\RequirePackage{foo}\RequirePackage[draft]{graphics}` you must write `\PassOptionsToPackage{draft}{graphics} \RequirePackage{foo}`. (If `foo.sty` loads an option in conflict with what you want then you may have to look into altering its source.)
>
> These commands are useful for general users as well as class and package writers. For instance, suppose a user wants to load the `graphicx` package with

the option `draft` and also wants to use a class `foo` that loads the `graphicx` package, but without that option. The user could start their LaTeX file with `\PassOptionsToPackage{draft}{graphicx}\documentclass{foo}`.

`\ProcessOptions`

`\ProcessOptions*\@options`

> Execute the code for each option that the user has invoked. Include it in the class file as `\ProcessOptions\relax` (because of the existence of the starred command).
>
> Options come in two types. *Local options* have been specified for this particular package in the *options* argument of `\PassOptionsToPackage{options}`, `\usepackage[options]`, or `\RequirePackage[options]`. *Global options* are those given by the class user in `\documentclass[options]` (If an option is specified both locally and globally then it is local.)
>
> When `\ProcessOptions` is called for a package `pkg.sty`, the following happens:
>
> 1. For each option *option* so far declared with `\DeclareOption`, it looks to see if that option is either a global or a local option for `pkg`. If so then it executes the declared code. This is done in the order in which these options were given in `pkg.sty`.
>
> 2. For each remaining local option, it executes the command `\ds@`*option* if it has been defined somewhere (other than by a `\DeclareOption`); otherwise, it executes the default option code given in `\DeclareOption*`. If no default option code has been declared then it gives an error message. This is done in the order in which these options were specified.
>
> When `\ProcessOptions` is called for a class it works in the same way except that all options are local, and the default *code* for `\DeclareOption*` is `\OptionNotUsed` rather than an error.
>
> The starred version `\ProcessOptions*` executes the options in the order specified in the calling commands, rather than in the order of declaration in the class or package. For a package this means that the global options are processed first.

`\ProvidesClass{class name}[release date brief additional information]`

`\ProvidesClass{class name}[release date]`

`\ProvidesPackage{package name}[release date brief additional information]`

`\ProvidesPackage{package name}[release date]`

> Identifies the class or package, printing a message to the screen and the log file.
>
> When a user writes `\documentclass{smcmemo}` then LaTeX loads the file `smcmemo.cls`. Similarly, a user writing `\usepackage{test}` prompts LaTeX to load the file `test.sty`. If the name of the file does not match the declared class or package name then you get a warning. Thus, if you invoke `\documentclass{smcmemo}`, and the file `smcmemo.cls` has the statement `\ProvidesClass{xxx}` then you get a warning like `You have requested document class 'smcmemo', but the document class provides 'xxx'`.
>
> This warning does not prevent LaTeX from processing the rest of the class file normally.
>
> If you include the optional argument, then you must include the date, before the first space if any, and it must have the form `YYYY/MM/DD`. The rest of the

optional argument is free-form, although it traditionally identifies the class, and is written to the screen during compilation and to the log file. Thus, if your file `smcmemo.cls` contains the line `\ProvidesClass{smcmemo}[2008/06/01 v1.0 SMC memo class]` and your document's first line is `\documentclass{smcmemo}` then you will see `Document Class: smcmemo 2008/06/01 v1.0 SMC memo class`.

The date in the optional argument allows class and package users to ask to be warned if the version of the class or package installed on their system is earlier than *release date*, by using the optional arguments such as `\documentclass{smcmemo}[2018/10/12]` or `\usepackage{foo}[[2017/07/07]]`. (Note that package users only rarely include a date, and class users almost never do.)

`\ProvidesFile{`*file name*`}[`*additional information*`]`

Declare a file other than the main class and package files, such as configuration files or font definition files. Put this command in that file and you get in the log a string like `File: test.config 2017/10/12 config file for test.cls` for *file name* equal to '`test.config`' and *additional information* equal to '`2017/10/12 config file for test.cls`'.

`\RequirePackage[`*option list*`]{`*package name*`}[`*release date*`]`
`\RequirePackageWithOptions{`*package name*`}[`*release date*`]`

Load a package, like the document author command `\usepackage`. See Section 3.2 [Additional packages], page 9. An example is `\RequirePackage[landscape,margin=1in]{geometry}`. Note that the LaTeX development team strongly recommends use of these commands over Plain TeX's `\input`; see the Class Guide.

The *option list*, if present, is a comma-separated list. The *release date*, if present, must have the form *YYYY/MM/DD*. If the release date of the package as installed on your system is earlier than *release date* then you get a warning like `You have requested, on input line 9, version '2017/07/03' of package jhtest, but only version '2000/01/01' is available`.

The `\RequirePackageWithOptions` version uses the list of options for the current class. This means it ignores any options passed to it via `\PassOptionsToClass`. This is a convenience command to allow easily building classes on existing ones without having to track which options were passed.

The difference between `\usepackage` and `\RequirePackage` is small. The `\usepackage` command is intended for the document file while `\RequirePackage` is intended for package and class files. Thus, using `\usepackage` before the `\documentclass` command causes LaTeX to give error like `\usepackage before \documentclass`, but you can use `\RequirePackage` there.

4 Fonts

Two important aspects of selecting a *font* are specifying a size and a style. The LaTeX commands for doing this are described here.

4.1 Font styles

The following type style commands are supported by LaTeX.

This first group of commands is typically used with an argument, as in `\textit{text}`. In the table below, the corresponding command in parenthesis is the "declaration form", which takes no arguments, as in `{\itshape text}`. The scope of the declaration form lasts until the next type style command or the end of the current group.

These commands, in both the argument form and the declaration form, are cumulative; e.g., you can say either `\sffamily\bfseries` or `\bfseries\sffamily` to get bold sans serif.

You can alternatively use an environment form of the declarations; for instance, `\begin{ttfamily}...\end{ttfamily}`.

These font-switching commands automatically insert italic corrections if needed. (See Section 19.7 [\/], page 108, for the details of italic corrections.) Specifically, they insert the italic correction unless the following character is in the list `\nocorrlist`, which by default consists of a period and a comma. To suppress the automatic insertion of italic correction, use `\nocorr` at the start or end of the command argument, such as `\textit{\nocorr text}` or `\textsc{text \nocorr}`.

`\textrm (\rmfamily)`
> Roman.

`\textit (\itshape)`
> Italics.

`\textmd (\mdseries)`
> Medium weight (default).

`\textbf (\bfseries)`
> Boldface.

`\textup (\upshape)`
> Upright (default).

`\textsl (\slshape)`
> Slanted.

`\textsf (\sffamily)`
> Sans serif.

`\textsc (\scshape)`
> Small caps.

`\texttt (\ttfamily)`
> Typewriter.

`\textnormal (\normalfont)`
> Main document font.

Although it also changes fonts, the \emph{*text*} command is semantic, for text to be emphasized, and should not be used as a substitute for \textit. For example, \emph{*start text \emph{middle text} end text*} will result in the *start text* and *end text* in italics, but *middle text* will be in roman.

LaTeX also provides the following commands, which unconditionally switch to the given style, that is, are *not* cumulative. Also, they are used differently than the above commands: {*cmd*...} instead of *cmd*{...}. These are two unrelated constructs.

\bf   Switch to bold face.

\cal   Switch to calligraphic letters for math.

\it   Italics.

\rm   Roman.

\sc   Small caps.

\sf   Sans serif.

\sl   Slanted (oblique).

\tt   Typewriter (monospace, fixed-width).

The \em command is the unconditional version of \emph.

(Some people consider the unconditional font-switching commands, such as \tt, obsolete and that only the cumulative commands (\texttt) should be used. Others think that both sets of commands have their place and sometimes an unconditional font switch is precisely what you want; for one example, see Section 8.4 [description], page 40.)

The following commands are for use in math mode. They are not cumulative, so \mathbf{\mathit{*symbol*}} does not create a boldface and italic *symbol*; instead, it will just be in italics. This is because typically math symbols need consistent typographic treatment, regardless of the surrounding environment.

\mathrm   Roman, for use in math mode.

\mathbf   Boldface, for use in math mode.

\mathsf   Sans serif, for use in math mode.

\mathtt   Typewriter, for use in math mode.

\mathit
(\mit)   Italics, for use in math mode.

\mathnormal
             For use in math mode, e.g., inside another type style declaration.

\mathcal   Calligraphic letters, for use in math mode.

In addition, the command \mathversion{bold} can be used for switching to bold letters and symbols in formulas. \mathversion{normal} restores the default.

Finally, the command \oldstylenums{*numerals*} will typeset so-called "old-style" numerals, which have differing heights and depths (and sometimes widths) from the standard "lining" numerals, which all have the same height as upper-case letters. LaTeX's default fonts support this, and will respect \textbf (but not other styles; there are no italic old-style numerals in Computer Modern). Many other fonts have old-style numerals also; sometimes the textcomp package must be loaded, and sometimes package options are provided to make them the default. FAQ entry: http://www.tex.ac.uk/cgi-bin/texfaq2html?label=osf.

4.2 Font sizes

The following standard type size commands are supported by LaTeX. The table shows the command name and the corresponding actual font size used (in points) with the '10pt', '11pt', and '12pt' document size options, respectively (see Section 3.1 [Document class options], page 8).

Command	10pt	11pt	12pt
\tiny	5	6	6
\scriptsize	7	8	8
\footnotesize	8	9	10
\small	9	10	10.95
\normalsize (default)	10	10.95	12
\large	12	12	14.4
\Large	14.4	14.4	17.28
\LARGE	17.28	17.28	20.74
\huge	20.74	20.74	24.88
\Huge	24.88	24.88	24.88

The commands as listed here are "declaration forms". The scope of the declaration form lasts until the next type style command or the end of the current group. You can also use the environment form of these commands; for instance, \begin{tiny}...\end{tiny}.

4.3 Low-level font commands

These commands are primarily intended for writers of macros and packages. The commands listed here are only a subset of the available ones.

\fontencoding{encoding}

Select the font encoding, the encoding of the output font. There are a large number of valid encodings. The most common are OT1, Knuth's original encoding for Computer Modern (the default), and T1, also known as the Cork encoding, which has support for the accented characters used by the most widespread European languages (German, French, Italian, Polish and others), which allows TeX to hyphenate words containing accented letters.

\fontfamily{family}

Select the font family. The web page http://www.tug.dk/FontCatalogue/ provides one way to browse through many of the fonts easily used with LaTeX. Here are examples of some common families:

pag Avant Garde

fvs Bitstream Vera Sans

pbk Bookman

`bch`	Charter
`ccr`	Computer Concrete
`cmr`	Computer Modern
`pcr`	Courier
`phv`	Helvetica
`fi4`	Inconsolata
`lmr`	Latin Modern
`lmss`	Latin Modern Sans
`lmtt`	Latin Modern Typewriter
`pnc`	New Century Schoolbook
`ppl`	Palatino
`ptm`	Times
`uncl`	Uncial
`put`	Utopia
`pzc`	Zapf Chancery

`\fontseries{series}`

Select the font series. A *series* combines a *weight* and a *width*. Typically, a font supports only a few of the possible combinations. Some common combined series values include:

`m`	Medium (normal)
`b`	Bold
`c`	Condensed
`bc`	Bold condensed
`bx`	Bold extended

The possible values for weight, individually, are:

`ul`	Ultra light
`el`	Extra light
`l`	Light
`sl`	Semi light
`m`	Medium (normal)
`sb`	Semi bold
`b`	Bold
`eb`	Extra bold
`ub`	Ultra bold

The possible values for width, individually, are (the percentages are just guides and are not followed precisely by all fonts):

`uc`	Ultra condensed, 50%
`ec`	Extra condensed, 62.5%
`c`	Condensed, 75%

> **sc** Semi condensed, 87.5%
>
> **m** Medium, 100%
>
> **sx** Semi expanded, 112.5%
>
> **x** Expanded, 125%
>
> **ex** Extra expanded, 150%
>
> **ux** Ultra expanded, 200%

When forming the *series* string from the weight and width, drop the **m** that stands for medium weight or medium width, unless both weight and width are **m**, in which case use just one ('m').

\fontshape{*shape*}

Select font shape. Valid shapes are:

> **n** Upright (normal)
>
> **it** Italic
>
> **sl** Slanted (oblique)
>
> **sc** Small caps
>
> **ui** Upright italics
>
> **ol** Outline

The two last shapes are not available for most font families, and small caps are often missing as well.

\fontsize{*size*}{*skip*}

Set the font size and the line spacing. The unit of both parameters defaults to points (**pt**). The line spacing is the nominal vertical space between lines, baseline to baseline. It is stored in the parameter **\baselineskip**. The default **\baselineskip** for the Computer Modern typeface is 1.2 times the **\fontsize**. Changing **\baselineskip** directly is inadvisable since its value is reset every time a size change happens; see **\baselinestretch**, next.

\baselinestretch

LaTeX multiplies the line spacing by the value of the **\baselinestretch** parameter; the default factor is 1. A change takes effect when **\selectfont** (see below) is called. You can make line skip changes happen for the entire document by doing **\renewcommand{\baselinestretch}{2.0}** in the preamble.

However, the best way to double-space a document is to use the **setspace** package. In addition to offering a number of spacing options, this package keeps the line spacing single-spaced in places where that is typically desirable, such as footnotes and figure captions. See the package documentation.

\linespread{*factor*}

Equivalent to **\renewcommand{\baselinestretch}{*factor*}**, and therefore must be followed by **\selectfont** to have any effect. Best specified in the preamble, or use the **setspace** package, as just described.

\selectfont

The effects of the font commands described above do not happen until **\selectfont** is called, as in **\fontfamily{*familyname*}\selectfont**. It is often useful to put this in a macro:

`\newcommand*{\myfont}{\fontfamily{`*`familyname`*`}\selectfont}`

(see Section 12.1 [\newcommand & \renewcommand], page 72).

`\usefont{`*`enc`*`}{`*`family`*`}{`*`series`*`}{`*`shape`*`}`

The same as invoking \fontencoding, \fontfamily, \fontseries and \fontshape with the given parameters, followed by \selectfont. For example:

`\usefont{ot1}{cmr}{m}{n}`

5 Layout

Commands for controlling the general page layout.

5.1 \onecolumn

Start a new page and produce single-column output. If the document is given the class option `onecolumn` then this is the default behavior (see Section 3.1 [Document class options], page 8).

This command is fragile (see Section 12.9 [\protect], page 78).

5.2 \twocolumn

Synopses:

```
\twocolumn
\twocolumn[prelim one column text]
```

Start a new page and produce two-column output. If the document is given the class option `twocolumn` then this is the default (see Section 3.1 [Document class options], page 8).

If the optional *prelim one column text* argument is present, it is typeset in one-column mode before the two-column typesetting starts.

This command is fragile (see Section 12.9 [\protect], page 78).

These parameters control typesetting in two-column output:

`\columnsep`
> The distance between columns. The default is 35pt. Change it with a command such as `\setlength{\columnsep}{40pt}` You must change it before the two column environment starts; in the preamble is a good place.

`\columnseprule`
> The width of the rule between columns. The rule appears halfway between the two columns. The default is 0pt, meaning that there is no rule. Change it with a command such as `\setlength{\columnseprule}{0.4pt}`, before the two-column environment starts.

`\columnwidth`
> The width of a single column. In one-column mode this is equal to `\textwidth`. In two-column mode by default LaTeX sets the width of each of the two columns to be half of `\textwidth` minus `\columnsep`.

In a two-column document, the starred environments `table*` and `figure*` are two columns wide, whereas the unstarred environments `table` and `figure` take up only one column (see Section 8.10 [figure], page 44, and see Section 8.22 [table], page 55). LaTeX places starred floats at the top of a page. The following parameters control float behavior of two-column output.

`\dbltopfraction`
> The maximum fraction at the top of a two-column page that may be occupied by two-column wide floats. The default is 0.7, meaning that the height of a `table*` or `figure*` environment must not exceed $0.7\textheight$. If the

height of your starred float environment exceeds this then you can take one of the following actions to prevent it from floating all the way to the back of the document:

- Use the [tp] location specifier to tell LaTeX to try to put the bulky float on a page by itself, as well as at the top of a page.
- Use the [t!] location specifier to override the effect of \dbltopfraction for this particular float.
- Increase the value of \dbltopfraction to a suitably large number, to avoid going to float pages so soon.

You can redefine it, for instance with \renewcommand{\dbltopfraction}{0.9}.█

\dblfloatpagefraction

For a float page of two-column wide floats, this is the minimum fraction that must be occupied by floats, limiting the amount of blank space. LaTeX's default is 0.5. Change it with \renewcommand.

\dblfloatsep

On a float page of two-column wide floats, this length is the distance between floats, at both the top and bottom of the page. The default is 12pt plus2pt minus2pt for a document set at 10pt or 11pt, and 14pt plus2pt minus4pt for a document set at 12pt.

\dbltextfloatsep

This length is the distance between a multi-column float at the top or bottom of a page and the main text. The default is 20pt plus2pt minus4pt.

\dbltopnumber

On a float page of two-column wide floats, this counter gives the maximum number of floats allowed at the top of the page. The LaTeX default is 2.

This example uses \twocolumn's optional argument of to create a title that spans the two-column article:

```
\documentclass[twocolumn]{article}
\newcommand{\authormark}[1]{\textsuperscript{#1}}
\begin{document}
\twocolumn[{% inside this optional argument goes one-column text
  \centering
  \LARGE The Title \\[1.5em]
  \large Author One\authormark{1},
         Author Two\authormark{2},
         Author Three\authormark{1} \\[1em]
  \normalsize
  \begin{tabular}{p{.2\textwidth}@{\hspace{2em}}p{.2\textwidth}}
    \authormark{1}Department one  &\authormark{2}Department two \\
    School one                    &School two
  \end{tabular}\\[3em] % space below title part
  }]

Two column text here.
```

5.3 \flushbottom

Make all pages in the documents after this declaration have the same height, by stretching the vertical space where necessary to fill out the page. This is most often used when making two-sided documents since the differences in facing pages can be glaring.

If TeX cannot satisfactorily stretch the vertical space in a page then you get a message like 'Underfull \vbox (badness 10000) has occurred while \output is active'. If you get that, one option is to change to \raggedbottom (see Section 5.4 [\raggedbottom], page 25). Alternatively, you can adjust the textheight to make compatible pages, or you can add some vertical stretch glue between lines or between paragraphs, as in \setlength{\parskip}{0ex plus0.1ex}. Your last option is to, in a final editing stage, adjust the height of individual pages (see Section 10.4 [\enlargethispage], page 67).

The \flushbottom state is the default only if you select the twoside document class option (see Section 3.1 [Document class options], page 8).

5.4 \raggedbottom

Make all later pages the natural height of the material on that page; no rubber vertical lengths will be stretched. Thus, in a two-sided document the facing pages may be different heights. This command can go at any point in the document body. See Section 5.3 [\flushbottom], page 25.

This is the default unless you select the twoside document class option (see Section 3.1 [Document class options], page 8).

5.5 Page layout parameters

\columnsep
\columnseprule
\columnwidth

> The distance between the two columns, the width of a rule between the columns, and the width of the columns, when the document class option twocolumn is in effect (see Section 3.1 [Document class options], page 8). See Section 5.2 [\twocolumn], page 23.

\headheight

> Height of the box that contains the running head. The default in the article, report, and book classes is '12pt', at all type sizes.

\headsep   Vertical distance between the bottom of the header line and the top of the main text. The default in the article and report classes is '25pt'. In the book class the default is: if the document is set at 10pt then it is '0.25in', and at 11pt and 12pt it is '0.275in'.

\footskip

> Distance from the baseline of the last line of text to the baseline of the page footer. The default in the article and report classes is '30pt'. In the book class the default is: when the type size is 10pt the default is '0.35in', while at 11pt it is '0.38in', and at 12pt it is '30pt'.

`\linewidth`

Width of the current line, decreased for each nested `list` (see Section 8.16 [list], page 48). That is, the nominal value for `\linewidth` is to equal `\textwidth` but for each nested list the `\linewidth` is decreased by the sum of that list's `\leftmargin` and `\rightmargin` (see Section 8.14 [itemize], page 46).

`\marginparpush`
`\marginsep`
`\marginparwidth`

The minimum vertical space between two marginal notes, the horizontal space between the text body and the marginal notes, and the horizontal width of the notes.

Normally marginal notes appear on the outside of the page, but the declaration `\reversemarginpar` changes that (and `\normalmarginpar` changes it back).

The defaults for `\marginparpush` in both **book** and **article** classes are: '7pt' if the document is set at 12pt, and '5pt' if the document is set at 11pt or 10pt.

For `\marginsep`, in **article** class the default is '10pt' except if the document is set at 10pt and in two-column mode where the default is '11pt'.

For `\marginsep` in **book** class the default is '10pt' in two-column mode and '7pt' in one-column mode.

For `\marginparwidth` in both **book** and **article** classes, in two-column mode the default is 60% of `\paperwidth` − `\textwidth`, while in one-column mode it is 50% of that distance.

`\oddsidemargin`
`\evensidemargin`

The `\oddsidemargin` is the extra distance between the left side of the page and the text's left margin, on odd-numbered pages when the document class option **twoside** is chosen and on all pages when **oneside** is in effect. When **twoside** is in effect, on even-numbered pages the extra distance on the left is evensidemargin.

LaTeX's default is that `\oddsidemargin` is 40% of the difference between `\paperwidth` and `\textwidth`, and `\evensidemargin` is the remainder.

`\paperheight`

The height of the paper, as distinct from the height of the print area. It is normally set with a document class option, as in `\documentclass[a4paper]{article}` (see Section 3.1 [Document class options], page 8).

`\paperwidth`

The width of the paper, as distinct from the width of the print area. It is normally set with a document class option, as in `\documentclass[a4paper]{article}` (see Section 3.1 [Document class options], page 8).

`\textheight`

The normal vertical height of the page body. If the document is set at a nominal type size of 10pt then for an **article** or **report** the default is

'43\baselineskip', while for a book it is '41\baselineskip'. At a type size of 11pt the default is '38\baselineskip' for all document classes. At 12pt it is '36\baselineskip' for all classes.

\textwidth

The full horizontal width of the entire page body. For an article or report document, the default is '345pt' when the chosen type size is 10pt, the default is '360pt' at 11pt, and it is '390pt' at 12pt. For a book document, the default is '4.5in' at a type size of 10pt, and '5in' at 11pt or 12pt.

In multi-column output, \textwidth remains the width of the entire page body, while \columnwidth is the width of one column (see Section 5.2 [\twocolumn], page 23).

In lists (see Section 8.16 [list], page 48), \textwidth remains the width of the entire page body (and \columnwidth the width of the entire column), while \linewidth may decrease for nested lists.

Inside a minipage (see Section 8.18 [minipage], page 49) or \parbox (see Section 20.5 [\parbox], page 112), all the width-related parameters are set to the specified width, and revert to their normal values at the end of the minipage or \parbox.

This entry is included for completeness: \hsize is the TEX primitive parameter used when text is broken into lines. It should not be used in normal LaTeX documents.

\topmargin

Space between the top of the TEX page (one inch from the top of the paper, by default) and the top of the header. The value is computed based on many other parameters: \paperheight − 2in − \headheight − \headsep − \textheight − \footskip, and then divided by two.

\topskip Minimum distance between the top of the page body and the baseline of the first line of text. For the standard classes, the default is the same as the font size, e.g., '10pt' at a type size of 10pt.

5.6 Floats

Some typographic elements, such as figures and tables, cannot be broken across pages. They must be typeset outside of the normal flow of text, for instance floating to the top of a later page.

LaTeX can have a number of different classes of floating material. The default is the two classes, figure (see Section 8.10 [figure], page 44) and table (see Section 8.22 [table], page 55), but you can create a new class with the package float.

Within any one float class LaTeX always respects the order, so that the first figure in a document source must be typeset before the second figure. However, LaTeX may mix the classes, so it can happen that while the first table appears in the source before the first figure, it appears in the output after it.

The placement of floats is subject to parameters, given below, that limit the number of floats that can appear at the top of a page, and the bottom, etc. If so many floats are queued that the limits prevent them all from fitting on a page then LaTeX places what it can and defers the rest to the next page. In this way, floats may end up being typeset far from their place in the source. In particular, a float that is big may migrate to the end of the document. In which event, because all floats in a class must appear in sequential order, every following float in that class also appears at the end.

In addition to changing the parameters, for each float you can tweak where the float placement algorithm tries to place it by using its *placement* argument. The possible values are a sequence of the letters below. The default for both `figure` and `table`, in both `article` and `book` classes, is `tbp`.

t   (Top)—at the top of a text page.

b   (Bottom)—at the bottom of a text page. (However, `b` is not allowed for full-width floats (`figure*`) with double-column output. To ameliorate this, use the `stfloats` or `dblfloatfix` package, but see the discussion at caveats in the FAQ: `http://www.tex.ac.uk/cgi-bin/texfaq2html?label=2colfloat`.

h   (Here)—at the position in the text where the `figure` environment appears. However, `h` is not allowed by itself; `t` is automatically added.

            To absolutely force a float to appear "here", you can `\usepackage{float}` and use the `H` specifier which it defines. For further discussion, see the FAQ entry at `http://www.tex.ac.uk/cgi-bin/texfaq2html?label=figurehere`.

p   (Page of floats)—on a separate *float page*, which is a page containing no text, only floats.

!   Used in addition to one of the above; for this float only, LaTeX ignores the restrictions on both the number of floats that can appear and the relative amounts of float and non-float text on the page. The ! specifier does *not* mean "put the float here"; see above.

Note: the order in which letters appear in the *placement* argument does not change the order in which LaTeX tries to place the float; for instance, `btp` has the same effect as `tbp`. All that *placement* does is that if a letter is not present then the algorithm does not try that location. Thus, LaTeX's default of `tbp` is to try every location except placing the float where it occurs in the source.

To prevent LaTeX from moving floats to the end of the document or a chapter you can use a `\clearpage` command to start a new page and insert all pending floats. If a pagebreak is undesirable then you can use the `afterpage` package and issue `\afterpage{\clearpage}`. This will wait until the current page is finished and then flush all outstanding floats.

LaTeX can typeset a float before where it appears in the source (although on the same output page) if there is a `t` specifier in the *placement* parameter. If this is not desired, and deleting the `t` is not acceptable as it keeps the float from being placed at the top of the next page, then you can prevent it by either using the `flafter` package or using the command `\suppressfloats[t]`, which causes floats for the top position on this page to moved to the next page.

Parameters relating to fractions of pages occupied by float and non-float text (change them with `\renewcommand{parameter}{decimal between 0 and 1}`):

`\bottomfraction`

> The maximum fraction of the page allowed to be occupied by floats at the bottom; default '.3'.

`\floatpagefraction`

> The minimum fraction of a float page that must be occupied by floats; default '.5'.

`\textfraction`

> Minimum fraction of a page that must be text; if floats take up too much space to preserve this much text, floats will be moved to a different page. The default is '.2'.

`\topfraction`

> Maximum fraction at the top of a page that may be occupied before floats; default '.7'.

Parameters relating to vertical space around floats (change them with `\setlength{`*parameter*`}{`*length expression*`}`):

`\floatsep`

> Space between floats at the top or bottom of a page; default '12pt plus2pt minus2pt'.

`\intextsep`

> Space above and below a float in the middle of the main text; default '12pt plus2pt minus2pt' for 10 point and 11 point documents, and '14pt plus4pt minus4pt' for 12 point documents.

`\textfloatsep`

> Space between the last (first) float at the top (bottom) of a page; default '20pt plus2pt minus4pt'.

Counters relating to the number of floats on a page (change them with `\setcounter{`*ctrname*`}{`*natural number*`}`):

`bottomnumber`

> Maximum number of floats that can appear at the bottom of a text page; default 1.

`dbltopnumber`

> Maximum number of full-sized floats that can appear at the top of a two-column page; default 2.

`topnumber`

> Maximum number of floats that can appear at the top of a text page; default 2.

`totalnumber`

> Maximum number of floats that can appear on a text page; default 3.

The principal TeX FAQ entry relating to floats `http://www.tex.ac.uk/cgi-bin/ texfaq2html?label=floats` contains suggestions for relaxing LaTeX's default parameters to reduce the problem of floats being pushed to the end. A full explanation of the float placement algorithm is in Frank Mittelbach's article "How to influence the position of float environments like figure and table in LaTeX?" (`http://latex-project.org/papers/tb111mitt-float.pdf`).

6 Sectioning

Sectioning commands provide the means to structure your text into units:

`\part`

`\chapter`   (`report` and `book` class only)

`\section`

`\subsection`
`\subsubsection`
`\paragraph`
`\subparagraph`

All sectioning commands take the same general form, e.g.,

> `\chapter[toctitle]{title}`

In addition to providing the heading *title* in the main text, the section title can appear in two other places:

1. The table of contents.
2. The running head at the top of the page.

You may not want the same text in these places as in the main text. To handle this, the sectioning commands have an optional argument *toctitle* that, when given, specifies the text for these other places.

Also, all sectioning commands have *-forms that print *title* as usual, but do not include a number and do not make an entry in the table of contents. For instance:

> `\section*{Preamble}`

The `\appendix` command changes the way following sectional units are numbered. The `\appendix` command itself generates no text and does not affect the numbering of parts. The normal use of this command is something like

> `\chapter{A Chapter}`
> `...`
> `\appendix`
> `\chapter{The First Appendix}`

The `secnumdepth` counter controls printing of section numbers. The setting

> `\setcounter{secnumdepth}{level}`

suppresses heading numbers at any depth > *level*, where `chapter` is level zero. (See Section 13.4 [\setcounter], page 82.)

6.1 \@startsection

Synopsis:

> `\@startsection{name}{level}{indent}{beforeskip}{afterskip}{style}`

Redefine the behavior of commands that start sectioning divisions such as `\section` or `\subsection`.

Note that the `titlesec` package makes manipulation of sectioning easier. Further, while most requirements for sectioning commands can be satisfied with `\@startsection`, some cannot. For instance, in the standard LaTeX `book` and `report` classes the commands `\chapter` and `\report` are not constructed in this way. To make such a command you may want to use the `\secdef` command.

Technically, this command has the form:

> `\@startsection{name}{level}{indent}{beforeskip}{afterskip}{style}`
> `*[toctitle]{title}`

so that issuing:

> `\renewcommand{\section}{\@startsection{name}{level}{indent}%`
> `{beforeskip}{afterskip}{style}}`

redefine `\section` while keeping its standard calling form `\section*[toctitle]{title}`. See Chapter 6 [Sectioning], page 31, and the examples below.

name   Name of the counter (which must be defined separately) used to number for the sectioning header. Most commonly either `section`, `subsection`, or `paragraph`. Although in those three cases the name of the counter is also the name of the sectioning command itself, using the same name is not required.

Then `\the`*name* displays the title number and `\`*name*`mark` is for the page headers.

level   An integer giving the depth of the sectioning command: 0 for `chapter` (only applies to the standard `book` and `report` classes), 1 for `section`, 2 for `subsection`, 3 for `subsubsection`, 4 for `paragraph`, and 5 for `subparagraph`. In the `book` and `report` classes `part` has level -1, while in the `article` class `part` has level 0.

If *level* is less than or equal to the value of `secnumdepth` then the titles for this sectioning command will be numbered. For instance, in an `article`, if `secnumdepth` is 1 then a `\section{Introduction}` command will produce output like `1 Introduction` while `\subsection{History}` will produce output like `History`, without the number prefix. See [Sectioning/secnumdepth], page 31.

If *level* is less than or equal to the value of *tocdepth* then the table of contents will have an entrie for this sectioning unit. For instance, in an `article`, if *tocdepth* is 1 then the table of contents will list sections but not subsections.

indent   A length giving the indentation of all of the title lines with respect to the left margin. To have the title flush with the margin use `0pt`. A negative indentation such as `-1em` will move the title into the left margin.

beforeskip   The absolute value of this length is the amount of vertical space that is inserted before this sectioning unit's title. This space will be discarded if the sectioning unit happens to start at the top of a fresh page. If this number is negative then the first paragraph following the header is not indented, if it is non-negative then the first paragraph is indented. (Note that the negative of `1pt plus 2pt minus 3pt` is `-1pt plus -2pt minus -3pt`.)

For example, if *beforeskip* is `-3.5ex plus -1ex minus -0.2ex` then to start the new sectioning unit, LaTeX will add about 3.5 times the height of a letter x in vertical space, and the first paragraph in the section will not be indented.

Using a rubber length, with `plus` and `minus`, is good practice here since it gives LaTeX more flexibility in making up the page.

The full accounting of the vertical space between the baseline of the line prior to this sectioning unit's header and the baseline of the header is that it is the sum of the `\parskip` of the text font, the `\baselineskip` of the title font, and the absolute value of the *beforeskip*. This space is typically rubber so it may stretch or shrink. (If the sectioning unit starts on a fresh page so that the vertical space is discarded then the baseline of the header text will be where LaTeX would put the baseline of the first text line on that page.)

afterskip   This is a length. If *afterskip* is non-negative then this is the vertical space inserted after the sectioning unit's title header. If it is negative then the title header becomes a run-in header, so that it becomes part of the next paragraph. In this case the absolute value of the length gives the horizontal space between the end of the title and the beginning of the following paragraph. (Note that the negative of `1pt plus 2pt minus 3pt` is `-1pt plus -2pt minus -3pt`.)

As with *beforeskip*, using a rubber length with `plus` and `minus` components is good practice here since it gives LaTeX more flexibility in putting the page together.

If `afterskip` is non-negative then the full accounting of the vertical space between the baseline of the sectioning unit's header and the baseline of the first line of the following paragraph is that it is the sum of the `\parskip` of the title font, the `\baselineskip` of the text font, and the value of *after*. That space is typically rubber so it may stretch or shrink. (Note that because the sign of `afterskip` changes the sectioning unit header's from standalone to run-in, you cannot use a negative `afterskip` to cancel part of the `\parskip`.)

style   Controls the styling of the title. See the examples below. Typical commands to use here are `\centering`, `\raggedright`, `\normalfont`, `\hrule`, or `\newpage`. The last command in *style* may be one such as `\MakeUppercase` or `\fbox` that takes one argument. The section title will be supplied as the argument to this command. For instance, setting *style* to `\bfseries\MakeUppercase` would produce titles that are bold and upper case.

Here are examples. To use them, either put them in a package or class file, or put them in the preamble of a LaTeX document between a `\makeatletter` command and a `\makeatother`. (Probably the error message `You can't use '\spacefactor' in vertical mode.` means that you forgot this.) See Section 2.4.3 [\makeatletter and \makeatother], page 6.

This will put section titles in large boldface type, centered.

```
\renewcommand\section{%
  \@startsection{section}% [name], page 32.
    {1}% [level], page 32.
    {0pt}% [indent], page 32.
    {-3.5ex plus -1ex minus -.2ex}% [beforeskip], page 32.
    {2.3ex plus.2ex}% [afterskip], page 33.
    {\centering\normalfont\Large\bfseries}% [style], page 33.
```

```
    }
```

This will put `subsection` titles in small caps type, inline with the paragraph.

```
\renewcommand\subsection{%
  \@startsection{subsection}%   [name], page 32.
    {2}%  [level], page 32.
    {0em}%  [indent], page 32.
    {-1ex plus 0.1ex minus -0.05ex}%  [beforeskip], page 32.
    {-1em plus 0.2em}%  [afterskip], page 33.
    {\scshape}%  [style], page 33.
  }
```

The prior examples redefined existing sectional unit title commands. This defines a new one, illustrating the needed counter and macros to display that counter.

```
\setcounter{secnumdepth}{6}% show counters this far down
\newcounter{subsubparagraph}[subparagraph]% counter for numbering
\renewcommand{\thesubsubparagraph}%                 how to display
  {\thesubparagraph.\@arabic\c@subsubparagraph}%  numbering
\newcommand{\subsubparagraph}{\@startsection
                    {subsubparagraph}%
                    {6}%
                    {0em}%
                    {\baselineskip}%
                    {0.5\baselineskip}%
                    {\normalfont\normalsize}}
\newcommand*\l@subsubparagraph{\@dottedtocline{6}{10em}{5em}}% for toc
\newcommand{\subsubparagraphmark}[1]{}% for page headers
```

7 Cross references

One reason for numbering things such as figures and equations is to refer the reader to them, as in "See Figure~3 for more details."

Including the figure number in the source is poor practice since if that number changes as the document evolves then you must remember to update this reference by hand. Instead, LaTeX has you write a *label* like `\label{eq:GreensThm}` and refer to it with `See equation~\ref{eq:GreensThm}`.

LaTeX writes the information from the labels to a file with the same name as the file containing the `\label{...}` but with an `.aux` extension. (The information has the format `\newlabel{label}{{currentlabel}{pagenumber}}` where *currentlabel* is the current value of the macro `\@currentlabel` that is usually updated whenever you call `\refstepcounter{counter}`.)

The most common side effect of the prior paragraph happens when your document has a *forward* reference, a `\ref{key}` that appears earlier than the associated `\label{key}`; see the example in the `\pageref{...}` description. LaTeX gets the information for references from the `.aux` file. If this is the first time you are compiling the document then you will get a message `LaTeX Warning: Label(s) may have changed. Rerun to get cross references right.` and in the output the reference will appear as two question marks '??', in boldface. Or, if you change some things so the references change then you get the same warning and the output contains the old reference information. The solution in either case is just to compile the document a second time.

7.1 \label

Synopsis:

> `\label{key}`

Assign a reference number to *key*. In ordinary text `\label{key}` assigns to *key* the number of the current sectional unit. Inside an environment with numbering, such as a `table` or `theorem` environment, `\label{key}` assigns to *key* the number of that environment. Retrieve the assigned number with the `\ref{key}` command (see Section 7.3 [\ref], page 36).

A key name can consist of any sequence of letters, digits, or common punctuation characters. Upper and lowercase letters are distinguished, as usual.

A common convention is to use labels consisting of a prefix and a suffix separated by a colon or period. This helps to avoid accidentally creating two labels with the same name, and makes your source more readable. Some commonly-used prefixes:

ch	for chapters
sec	for lower-level sectioning commands
fig	for figures
tab	for tables
eq	for equations

Thus, `\label{fig:Euler}` is a label for a figure with a portrait of the great man.

In this example below the key `sec:test` will get the number of the current section and the key `fig:test` will get the number of the figure. (Incidentally, put labels after captions in figures and tables.)

```
\section{section name}
\label{sec:test}
This is Section~\ref{sec:test}.
\begin{figure}
  ...
  \caption{caption text}
  \label{fig:test}
\end{figure}
See Figure~\ref{fig:test}.
```

7.2 `\pageref{`*key*`}`

Synopsis:

```
\pageref{key}
```

Produce the page number of the place in the text where the corresponding `\label{`*key*`}` command appears.

In this example the `\label{eq:main}` is used both for the formula number and for the page number. (Note that the two references are forward references, so this document would need to be compiled twice to resolve those.)

```
The main result is formula~\ref{eq:main} on page~\pageref{eq:main}.
  ...
\begin{equation} \label{eq:main}
  \mathbf{P}=\mathbf{NP}
\end{equation}
```

7.3 `\ref{`*key*`}`

Synopsis:

```
\ref{key}
```

Produces the number of the sectional unit, equation, footnote, figure, ..., of the corresponding `\label` command (see Section 7.1 [\label], page 35). It does not produce any text, such as the word 'Section' or 'Figure', just the bare number itself.

In this example, the `\ref{popular}` produces '2'. Note that it is a forward reference since it comes before `\label{popular}`.

```
The most widely-used format is item number~\ref{popular}.
\begin{enumerate}
\item Plain \TeX
\item \label{popular} \LaTeX
\item Con\TeX t
\end{enumerate}
```

8 Environments

LaTeX provides many environments for delimiting certain behavior. An environment begins with \begin and ends with \end, like this:

```
\begin{environment-name}
  ...
\end{environment-name}
```

The *environment-name* at the beginning must exactly match that at the end. For instance, the input \begin{table*}...\end{table} will cause an error like: '! LaTeX Error: \begin{table*} on input line 5 ended by \end{table}.'

Environments are executed within a group.

8.1 abstract

Synopsis:

```
\begin{abstract}
...
\end{abstract}
```

Produce an abstract, possibly of multiple paragraphs. This environment is only defined in the **article** and **report** document classes (see Chapter 3 [Document classes], page 8).

Using the example below in the **article** class produces a displayed paragraph. Document class option **titlepage** causes the abstract to be on a separate page (see Section 3.1 [Document class options], page 8); this is the default only in the **report** class.

```
\begin{abstract}
  We compare all known accounts of the proposal made by Porter Alexander
  to Robert E Lee at the Appomattox Court House that the army continue
  in a guerrilla war, which Lee refused.
\end{abstract}
```

The next example produces a one column abstract in a two column document (for a more flexible solution, use the package **abstract**).

```
\documentclass[twocolumn]{article}
  ...
\begin{document}
\title{Babe Ruth as Cultural Progenitor: a Atavistic Approach}
\author{Smith \\ Jones \\ Robinson\thanks{Railroad tracking grant.}}
\twocolumn[
  \begin{@twocolumnfalse}
    \maketitle
    \begin{abstract}
      Ruth was not just the Sultan of Swat, he was the entire swat
      team.
    \end{abstract}
  \end{@twocolumnfalse}
  ]
{   % by-hand insert a footnote at page bottom
```

```
\renewcommand{\thefootnote}{\fnsymbol{footnote}}
\footnotetext[1]{Thanks for all the fish.}
}
```

8.2 array

Synopsis:

```
\begin{array}{cols}
  column 1 entry &column 2 entry ... &column n entry \\
  ...
\end{array}
```

or

```
\begin{array}[pos]{cols}
  column 1 entry &column 2 entry ... &column n entry \\
  ...
\end{array}
```

Produce a mathematical array. This environment can only be used in math mode, and normally appears within a displayed mathematics environment such as `equation` (see Section 8.9 [equation], page 44). Column entries are separated by an ampersand (`&`). Rows are terminated with double-backslashes (see Section 9.1 [\\], page 65).

The required argument *cols* describes the number of columns, their alignment, and the formatting of the intercolumn regions. See Section 8.23 [tabular], page 56, for the complete description of *cols*, and of the other common features of the two environments, including the optional *pos* argument.

There are two ways that `array` diverges from `tabular`. The first is that `array` entries are typeset in math mode, in textstyle (except if the *cols* definition specifies the column with `p{...}`, which causes the entry to be typeset in text mode). The second is that, instead of `tabular`'s parameter `\tabcolsep`, LaTeX's intercolumn space in an `array` is governed by `\arraycolsep`, which gives half the width between columns. The default for this is '`5pt`'.

To obtain arrays with braces the standard is to use the `amsmath` package. It comes with environments `pmatrix` for an array surrounded by parentheses (`...`), `bmatrix` for an array surrounded by square brackets [`...`], `Bmatrix` for an array surrounded by curly braces {`...`}, `vmatrix` for an array surrounded by vertical bars |`...`|, and `Vmatrix` for an array surrounded by double vertical bars ||`...`||, along with a number of other array constructs.

Here is an example of an array:

```
\begin{equation}
  \begin{array}{cr}
    \sqrt{y}  &12.3 \\
    x^2       &3.4
  \end{array}
\end{equation}
```

The next example works if `\usepackage{amsmath}` is in the preamble:

```
\begin{equation}
  \begin{vmatrix}{cc}
```

```
    a   &b \\
    c   &d
  \end{vmatrix}=ad-bc
\end{equation}
```

8.3 center

Synopsis:

```
\begin{center}
  ... text ...
\end{center}
```

Create a new paragraph consisting of a sequence of lines that are centered within the left and right margins on the current page. Use double-backslash to get a line break at a particular spot (see Section 9.1 [\\], page 65). If some text environment body is too long to fit on a line, LaTeX will insert line breaks that avoid hyphenation and avoid stretching or shrinking any interword space.

This environment inserts space above and below the text body. See Section 8.3.1 [\centering], page 39, to avoid such space, for example inside a figure environment.

This example produces three centered lines. There is extra vertical space between the last two lines.

```
\begin{center}
  A Thesis Submitted in Partial Fufillment \\
  of the Requirements of \\[0.5ex]
  the School of Environmental Engineering
\end{center}
```

In this example, depending on the page's line width, LaTeX may choose a line break for the part before the double backslash. If so, it will center each of the two lines and if not it will center the single line. Then LaTeX will break at the double backslash, and will center the ending.

```
\begin{center}
  My father considered that anyone who went to chapel and didn't drink
  alcohol was not to be tolerated.\\
  I grew up in that belief.  --Richard Burton
\end{center}
```

A double backslash after the final line is optional.

8.3.1 \centering

A declaration that causes material in its scope to be centered. It is most often used inside an environment such as figure, or in a parbox.

Unlike the center environment, the \centering command does not add vertical space above and below the text.

It also does not start a new paragraph; it simply changes how LaTeX formats paragraph units. If ww {\centering xx \\ yy} zz is surrounded by blank lines then LaTeX will create a paragraph whose first line 'ww xx' is centered and whose second line, not centered, contains 'yy zz'. Usually what is desired is for the scope of the declaration to contain a blank line or the `\end` command of an environment such as `figure` or `table` that ends the paragraph unit. Thus, if `{\centering xx \\ yy\par} zz` is surrounded by blank lines then it makes a new paragraph with two centered lines 'xx' and 'yy', followed by a new paragraph with 'zz' that is formatted as usual. See also the following example.

This example's `\centering` causes the graphic to be horizontally centered.

```
\begin{figure}
  \centering
  \includegraphics[width=0.6\textwidth]{ctan_lion.png}
  \caption{CTAN Lion}  \label{fig:CTANLion}
\end{figure}
```

The scope of the `\centering` ends with the `\end{figure}`.

8.4 description

Synopsis:

```
\begin{description}
\item [first label] text of first item
\item [second label] text of second item
  ...
\end{description}
```

Environment to make a labelled list of items. Each item's *label* is typeset in bold, flush-left. Each item's text may contain multiple paragraphs. Although the labels on the items are optional there is no sensible default, so all items should have labels.

The list consists of at least one item, created with the `\item` command (see Section 8.16.1 [\item], page 48). Having no items causes the LaTeX error 'Something's wrong--perhaps a missing \item').

Since the labels are in bold style, if the label text calls for a font change given in argument style (see Section 4.1 [Font styles], page 17) then it will come out bold. For instance, if the label text calls for typewriter with `\item[\texttt{label text}]` then it will appear in bold typewriter, if that is available. The simplest way to get non-bold typewriter is to use declarative style: `\item[{\tt label text}]`. Similarly, to get the standard roman font, use `\item[{\rm label text}]`.

For other major LaTeX labelled list environments, see Section 8.14 [itemize], page 46, and Section 8.7 [enumerate], page 42. For information about customizing list layout, see Section 8.16 [list], page 48; also, the package `enumitem` is useful for this.

This example shows the environment used for a sequence of definitions.

```
\begin{definition}
  \item[lama] A priest.
  \item[llama] A beast.
\end{definition}
```

8.5 displaymath

Synopsis:

```
\begin{displaymath}
```

```
math text
\end{displaymath}
```

Environment to typeset the math text on its own line, in display style and centered. To make the text be flush-left use the global option `fleqn`; see Section 3.1 [Document class options], page 8.

In the `displaymath` environment no equation number is added to the math text. One way to get an equation number is to use the `equation` environment (see Section 8.9 [equation], page 44).

LaTeX will not break the *math text* across lines.

Note that the `amsmath` package has significantly more extensive displayed equation facilities. For example, there are a number of ways in that package for having math text broken across lines.

The construct `\[`*math text*`\]` is essentially a synonym for `\begin{displaymath}`*math text*`\end{displaymath}` but the latter is easier to work with in the source file; for instance, searching for a square bracket may get false positives but the word `displaymath` will likely be unique. (The construct `$$`*math text*`$$` from Plain TeX is sometimes mistakenly used as a synonym for `displaymath`. It is not a synonym, because the `displaymath` environment checks that it isn't started in math mode and that it ends in math mode begun by the matching environment start, because the `displaymath` environment has different vertical spacing, and because the `displaymath` environment honors the `fleqn` option.)

The output from this example is centered and alone on its line.

```
\begin{displaymath}
  \int_1^2 x^2\,dx=7/3
\end{displaymath}
```

Also, the integral sign is larger than the inline version `\( \int_1^2 x^2\,dx=7/3 \)` produces.

8.6 document

The `document` environment encloses the entire body of a document. It is required in every LaTeX document. See Section 2.1 [Starting and ending], page 3.

Synopsis:

```
\AtBeginDocument{code}
```

Save *code* and execute it when `\begin{document}` is executed, at the very end of the preamble. The code is executed after the font selection tables have been set up, so the normal font for the document is the current font. However, the code is executed as part of the preamble so you cannot do any typesetting with it.

You can issue this command more than once; the successive code lines will be executed in the order that you gave them.

Synopsis:

```
\AtEndDocument{code}
```

Save *code* and execute it near the end of the document. Specifically, it is executed when `\end{document}` is executed, before the final page is finished and before any leftover floating environments are processed. If you want some of the code to be executed after these two processes then include a \clearpage at the appropriate point in *code*.

You can issue this command more than once; the successive code lines will be executed in the order that you gave them.

8.7 enumerate

Synopsis:

```
\begin{enumerate}
\item [first label] text of first item
\item [second label] text of second item
...
\end{enumerate}
```

Environment to produce a numbered list of items. The format of the label numbering depends on whether this environment is nested within another; see below.

The list consists of at least one item. Having no items causes the LaTeX error 'Something's wrong--perhaps a missing \item'. Each item is produced with an \item command.

This example lists the top two finishers in the 1908 Olympic marathon.

```
\begin{enumerate}
\item Johnny Hayes (USA)
\item Charles Hefferon (RSA)
\end{enumerate}
```

Enumerations may be nested within a paragraph-making environment, including **itemize** (see Section 8.14 [itemize], page 46), **description** (see Section 8.4 [description], page 40) and **enumeration**, up to four levels deep. The format of the label produced depends on the place in the nesting. This gives LaTeX's default for the format at each nesting level (where 1 is the outermost level):

1. arabic number followed by a period: '1.', '2.', ...
2. lower case letter inside parentheses: '(a)', '(b)' ...
3. lower case roman numeral followed by a period: 'i.', 'ii.', ...
4. upper case letter followed by a period: 'A.', 'B.', ...

The **enumerate** environment uses the counters \enumi through \enumiv counters (see Chapter 13 [Counters], page 80). If you use the optional argument to \item then the counter is not incremented for that item (see Section 8.16.1 [\item], page 48).

To change the format of the label use \renewcommand (see Section 12.1 [\newcommand & \renewcommand], page 72) on the commands \labelenumi through \labelenumiv. For instance, this first level list will be labelled with uppercase letters, in boldface, and without a trailing period:

```
\renewcommand{\labelenumi}{\textbf{\Alph{enumi}}}
\begin{enumerate}
  \item eI
  \item bi:
  \item si:
```

```
\end{enumerate}
```

For a list of counter-labelling commands like \Alph see Section 13.1 [\alph \Alph \arabic \roman \Roman \fnsymbol], page 80.

For more on customizing the layout see Section 8.16 [list], page 48. Also, the package enumitem is useful for this.

8.8 eqnarray

First, a caveat: the eqnarray environment is depreciated. It has infelicities that cannot be overcome, including spacing that is inconsistent with other mathematics elements (see the article "Avoid eqnarray!" by Lars Madsen http://tug.org/TUGboat/tb33-1/tb103madsen.pdf). New documents should include the amsmath package and use the displayed mathematics environments provided there, such as the align environment.

Nevertheless, for completeness and for a reference when working with old documents, a synopsis:

```
\begin{eqnarray}
  first formula left  &first formula middle  &first formula right \\
  ...
\end{eqnarray}
```

or

```
\begin{eqnarray*}
  first formula left  &first formula middle  &first formula right \\
  ...
\end{eqnarray*}
```

Display a sequence of equations or inequalities. The left and right sides are typeset in display mode, while the middle is typeset in text mode.

It is similar to a three-column array environment, with items within a row separated by an ampersand (&), and with rows separated by double backslash \\). The starred form of line break (*) can also be used to separate equations, and will disallow a page break there (see Section 9.1 [\\], page 65).

The unstarred form eqnarray places an equation number on every line (using the equation counter), unless that line contains a \nonumber command. The starred form eqnarray* omits equation numbering, while otherwise being the same.

The command \lefteqn is used for splitting long formulas across lines. It typesets its argument in display style flush left in a box of zero width.

This example shows three lines. The first two lines make an inequality, while the third line has not entry on the left side.

```
\begin{eqnarray*}
  \lefteqn{x_1+x_2+\cdots+x_n}      \\
    &\leq &y_1+y_2+\cdots+y_n       \\
    &=    &z+y_3+\cdots+y_n
\end{eqnarray*}
```

8.9 `equation`

Synopsis:

```
\begin{equation}
  math text
\end{equation}
```

Make a `displaymath` environment (see Section 8.5 [displaymath], page 40) with an equation number in the right margin.

The equation number is generated using the `equation` counter.

Note that the `amsmath` package has extensive displayed equation facilities. Those facilities are the best approach for such output in new documents.

8.10 `figure`

Synopsis:

```
\begin{figure}[placement]
  figure body
\caption[loftitle]{title}
\label{label}
\end{figure}
```

or

```
\begin{figure*}[placement]
  figure body
\caption[loftitle]{title}
\label{label}
\end{figure*}
```

A class of floats (see Section 5.6 [Floats], page 27). Because they cannot be split across pages, they are not typeset in sequence with the normal text but instead are "floated" to a convenient place, such as the top of a following page.

For the possible values of *placement* and their effect on the float placement algorithm, see Section 5.6 [Floats], page 27.

The starred form `figure*` is used when a document is in double-column mode (see Section 5.2 [\twocolumn], page 23). It produces a figure that spans both columns, at the top of the page. To add the possibility of placing at a page bottom see the discussion of *placement* b in Section 5.6 [Floats], page 27.

The figure body is typeset in a `parbox` of width `\textwidth` and so it can contain text, commands, etc.

The label is optional; it is used for cross references (see Chapter 7 [Cross references], page 35). The optional `\caption` command specifies caption text for the figure. By default it is numbered. If *loftitle* is present, it is used in the list of figures instead of *title* (see Section 23.1 [Tables of contents], page 122).

This example makes a figure out of a graphic. It requires one of the packages `graphics` or `graphicx`. The graphic, with its caption, will be placed at the top of a page or, if it is pushed to the end of the document, on a page of floats.

```
\begin{figure}[t]
```

```
    \centering
    \includegraphics[width=0.5\textwidth]{CTANlion.png}
    \caption{The CTAN lion, by Duane Bibby}
\end{figure}
```

8.11 filecontents: Write an external file

Synopsis:

```
\begin{filecontents}{filename}
  text
\end{filecontents}
```

or

```
\begin{filecontents*}{filename}
  text
\end{filecontents*}
```

Create a file named *filename* and fill it with *text*. The unstarred version of the environment `filecontents` prefixes the content of the created file with a header; see the example below. The starred version `filecontents*` does not include the header.

This environment can be used anywhere in the preamble, although it often appears before the `\documentclass` command. It is typically used when a source file requires a nonstandard style or class file. The environment will write that file to the directory containing the source and thus make the source file self-contained. Another use is to include `bib` references in the file, again to make it self-contained.

The environment checks whether a file of that name already exists and if so, does not do anything. There is a `filecontents` package that redefines the `filecontents` environment so that instead of doing nothing in that case, it will overwrite the existing file.

For example, this document

```
\documentclass{article}
\begin{filecontents}{JH.sty}
\newcommand{\myname}{Jim Hef{}feron}
\end{filecontents}
\usepackage{JH}
\begin{document}
Article by \myname.
\end{document}
```

produces this file JH.sty.

```
%% LaTeX2e file 'JH.sty'
%% generated by the 'filecontents' environment
%% from source 'test' on 2015/10/12.
%%
\newcommand{\myname}{Jim Hef{}feron}
```

8.12 flushleft

```
\begin{flushleft}
```

```
line1 \\
line2 \\
...
\end{flushleft}
```

The `flushleft` environment allows you to create a paragraph consisting of lines that are flush to the left-hand margin and ragged right. Each line must be terminated with the string \\.

8.12.1 \raggedright

The `\raggedright` declaration corresponds to the `flushleft` environment. This declaration can be used inside an environment such as `quote` or in a `parbox`.

Unlike the `flushleft` environment, the `\raggedright` command does not start a new paragraph; it only changes how LaTeX formats paragraph units. To affect a paragraph unit's format, the scope of the declaration must contain the blank line or `\end` command that ends the paragraph unit.

8.13 flushright

```
\begin{flushright}
line1 \\
line2 \\
...
\end{flushright}
```

The `flushright` environment allows you to create a paragraph consisting of lines that are flush to the right-hand margin and ragged left. Each line must be terminated with the control sequence \\.

8.13.1 \raggedleft

The `\raggedleft` declaration corresponds to the `flushright` environment. This declaration can be used inside an environment such as `quote` or in a `parbox`.

Unlike the `flushright` environment, the `\raggedleft` command does not start a new paragraph; it only changes how LaTeX formats paragraph units. To affect a paragraph unit's format, the scope of the declaration must contain the blank line or `\end` command that ends the paragraph unit.

8.14 itemize

Synopsis:

```
\begin{itemize}
\item item1
\item item2
...
\end{itemize}
```

The `itemize` environment produces an "unordered", "bulleted" list. Itemized lists can be nested within one another, up to four levels deep. They can also be nested within other paragraph-making environments, such as `enumerate` (see Section 8.7 [enumerate], page 42).

Each item of an `itemize` list begins with an `\item` command. There must be at least one `\item` command within the environment.

By default, the marks at each level look like this:

1. • (bullet)
2. -- (bold en-dash)
3. * (asterisk)
4. · (centered dot)

The `itemize` environment uses the commands `\labelitemi` through `\labelitemiv` to produce the default label. So, you can use `\renewcommand` to change the labels. For instance, to have the first level use diamonds:

> `\renewcommand{\labelitemi}{$\diamond$}`

The `\leftmargini` through `\leftmarginvi` parameters define the distance between the left margin of the enclosing environment and the left margin of the list. By convention, `\leftmargin` is set to the appropriate `\leftmarginN` when a new level of nesting is entered.

The defaults vary from '`.5em`' (highest levels of nesting) to '`2.5em`' (first level), and are a bit reduced in two-column mode. This example greatly reduces the margin space for outermost lists:

> `\setlength{\leftmargini}{1.25em} % default 2.5em`

Some parameters that affect list formatting:

`\itemindent`
> Extra indentation before each item in a list; default zero.

`\labelsep`
> Space between the label and text of an item; default '`.5em`'.

`\labelwidth`
> Width of the label; default '`2em`', or '`1.5em`' in two-column mode.

`\listparindent`
> Extra indentation added to second and subsequent paragraphs within a list item; default '`0pt`'.

`\rightmargin`
> Horizontal distance between the right margin of the list and the enclosing environment; default '`0pt`', except in the `quote`, `quotation`, and `verse` environments, where it is set equal to `\leftmargin`.

Parameters affecting vertical spacing between list items (rather loose, by default).

`\itemsep` Vertical space between items. The default is `2pt plus1pt minus1pt` for `10pt` documents, `3pt plus2pt minus1pt` for `11pt`, and `4.5pt plus2pt minus1pt` for `12pt`.

`\parsep` Extra vertical space between paragraphs within a list item. Defaults are the same as `\itemsep`.

`\topsep` Vertical space between the first item and the preceding paragraph. For top-level lists, the default is `8pt plus2pt minus4pt` for `10pt` documents, `9pt plus3pt` minus5pt for 11pt, and 10pt plus4pt minus6pt for 12pt. These are reduced for nested lists.

\partopsep

Extra space added to \topsep when the list environment starts a paragraph. The default is 2pt plus1pt minus1pt for 10pt documents, 3pt plus1pt minus1pt for 11pt, and 3pt plus2pt minus2pt for 12pt.

Especially for lists with short items, it may be desirable to elide space between items. Here is an example defining an itemize* environment with no extra spacing between items, or between paragraphs within a single item (\parskip is not list-specific, see Section 15.3 [\parskip], page 85):

```
\newenvironment{itemize*}%
  {\begin{itemize}%
    \setlength{\itemsep}{0pt}%
    \setlength{\parsep}{0pt}}%
    \setlength{\parskip}{0pt}}%
  {\end{itemize}}
```

8.15 letter environment: writing letters

This environment is used for creating letters. See Chapter 24 [Letters], page 124.

8.16 list

The list environment is a generic environment which is used for defining many of the more specific environments. It is seldom used in documents, but often in macros.

```
\begin{list}{labeling}{spacing}
\item item1
\item item2
...
\end{list}
```

The mandatory *labeling* argument specifies how items should be labelled (unless the optional argument is supplied to \item). This argument is a piece of text that is inserted in a box to form the label. It can and usually does contain other LaTeX commands.

The mandatory *spacing* argument contains commands to change the spacing parameters for the list. This argument will most often be empty, i.e., {}, which leaves the default spacing.

The width used for typesetting the list items is specified by \linewidth (see Section 5.5 [Page layout parameters], page 25).

8.16.1 \item: An entry in a list.

Synopsis:

```
\item text of item
```

or

```
\item[optional label] text of item
```

An entry in a list. The entries are prefixed by a label, whose default depends on the list type.

Because the optional argument *optional label* is surrounded by square brackets ([and]), to use square brackets inside the optional argument you must hide them inside curly braces, as in `\item[Close square bracket, {]}]`. Similarly, to use an open square bracket as first character in the text of the item, also hide it inside curly braces. See Section 2.4 [LaTeX command syntax], page 5.

In this example the **enumerate** list has two items that use the default label and one that uses the optional label.

```
\begin{enumerate}
  \item Moe
  \item[sometimes] Shemp
  \item Larry
\end{enumerate}
```

The first item is labelled '1.', the second item is labelled '**sometimes**', and the third item is labelled '2.' (note that, because of the optional label in the second item, the third item does not get a '3.').

8.17 math

Synopsis:

```
\begin{math}
math
\end{math}
```

The **math** environment inserts the given *math* within the running text. `\(...\)` and `$...$` are synonyms. See Chapter 16 [Math formulas], page 87.

8.18 minipage

```
\begin{minipage}[position][height][inner-pos]{width}
text
\end{minipage}
```

The **minipage** environment typesets its body *text* in a block that will not be broken across pages. This is similar to the `\parbox` command (see Section 20.5 [\parbox], page 112), but unlike `\parbox`, other paragraph-making environments can be used inside a minipage.

The arguments are the same as for `\parbox` (see Section 20.5 [\parbox], page 112).

By default, paragraphs are not indented in the **minipage** environment. You can restore indentation with a command such as `\setlength{\parindent}{1pc}` command.

Footnotes in a **minipage** environment are handled in a way that is particularly useful for putting footnotes in figures or tables. A `\footnote` or `\footnotetext` command puts the footnote at the bottom of the minipage instead of at the bottom of the page, and it uses the `\mpfootnote` counter instead of the ordinary **footnote** counter (see Chapter 13 [Counters], page 80).

However, don't put one minipage inside another if you are using footnotes; they may wind up at the bottom of the wrong minipage.

8.19 `picture`

```
\begin{picture}(width,height)(xoffset,yoffset)
... picture commands ...
\end{picture}
```

The `picture` environment allows you to create just about any kind of picture you want containing text, lines, arrows and circles. You tell LaTeX where to put things in the picture by specifying their coordinates. A coordinate is a number that may have a decimal point and a minus sign—a number like `5`, `0.3` or `-3.1416`. A coordinate specifies a length in multiples of the unit length `\unitlength`, so if `\unitlength` has been set to `1cm`, then the coordinate 2.54 specifies a length of 2.54 centimeters.

You should only change the value of `\unitlength`, using the `\setlength` command, outside of a `picture` environment. The default value is `1pt`.

The `picture` package redefine the `picture` environment so that everywhere a number is used in a *picture commands* to specify a coordinate, one can use alternatively a length. Be aware however that this will prevent scaling those lengths by changing `\unitlength`.

A *position* is a pair of coordinates, such as `(2.4,-5)`, specifying the point with x-coordinate `2.4` and y-coordinate `-5`. Coordinates are specified in the usual way with respect to an origin, which is normally at the lower-left corner of the picture. Note that when a position appears as an argument, it is not enclosed in braces; the parentheses serve to delimit the argument.

The `picture` environment has one mandatory argument which is a position (*width,height*), which specifies the size of the picture. The environment produces a rectangular box with these *width* and *height*.

The `picture` environment also has an optional position argument (*xoffset,yoffset*), following the size argument, that can change the origin. (Unlike ordinary optional arguments, this argument is not contained in square brackets.) The optional argument gives the coordinates of the point at the lower-left corner of the picture (thereby determining the origin). For example, if `\unitlength` has been set to `1mm`, the command

```
\begin{picture}(100,200)(10,20)
```

produces a picture of width 100 millimeters and height 200 millimeters, whose lower-left corner is the point (10,20) and whose upper-right corner is therefore the point (110,220). When you first draw a picture, you typically omit the optional argument, leaving the origin at the lower-left corner. If you then want to modify your picture by shifting everything, you can just add the appropriate optional argument.

The environment's mandatory argument determines the nominal size of the picture. This need bear no relation to how large the picture really is; LaTeX will happily allow you to put things outside the picture, or even off the page. The picture's nominal size is used by LaTeX in determining how much room to leave for it.

Everything that appears in a picture is drawn by the `\put` command. The command

```
\put (11.3,-.3){...}
```

puts the object specified by `...` in the picture, with its reference point at coordinates $(11.3, -.3)$. The reference points for various objects will be described below.

The \put command creates an *LR box*. You can put anything that can go in an \mbox (see Section 20.1 [\mbox], page 111) in the text argument of the \put command. When you do this, the reference point will be the lower left corner of the box.

The picture commands are described in the following sections.

8.19.1 \circle

Synopsis:

> \circle[*]{*diameter*}

The \circle command produces a circle with a diameter as close to the specified one as possible. The *-form of the command draws a solid circle.

Circles up to 40 pt can be drawn.

8.19.2 \makebox

Synopsis:

> \makebox(*width*,*height*)[*position*]{*text*}

The \makebox command for the picture environment is similar to the normal \makebox command except that you must specify a *width* and *height* in multiples of \unitlength.

The optional argument, [*position*], specifies the quadrant that your *text* appears in. You may select up to two of the following:

t   Moves the item to the top of the rectangle.

b   Moves the item to the bottom.

l   Moves the item to the left.

r   Moves the item to the right.

See Section 20.4 [\makebox], page 111.

8.19.3 \framebox

Synopsis:

> \framebox(*width*,*height*)[*pos*]{...}

The \framebox command is like \makebox (see previous section), except that it puts a frame around the outside of the box that it creates.

The \framebox command produces a rule of thickness \fboxrule, and leaves a space \fboxsep between the rule and the contents of the box.

8.19.4 \dashbox

Draws a box with a dashed line. Synopsis:

> \dashbox{*dlen*}(*rwidth*,*rheight*)[*pos*]{*text*}

\dashbox creates a dashed rectangle around *text* in a picture environment. Dashes are *dlen* units long, and the rectangle has overall width *rwidth* and height *rheight*. The *text* is positioned at optional *pos*.

A dashed box looks best when the *rwidth* and *rheight* are multiples of the *dlen*.

8.19.5 \frame

Synopsis:

> \frame{*text*}

The \frame command puts a rectangular frame around *text*. The reference point is the bottom left corner of the frame. No extra space is put between the frame and the object.

8.19.6 \line

Synopsis:

> \line(*xslope,yslope*){*length*}

The \line command draws a line with the given *length* and slope *xslope/yslope*.

Standard LaTeX can only draw lines with *slope* = x/y, where x and y have integer values from −6 through 6. For lines of any slope, and plenty of other shapes, see pict2e and many other packages on CTAN.

8.19.7 \linethickness

The \linethickness{*dim*} command declares the thickness of horizontal and vertical lines in a picture environment to be *dim*, which must be a positive length.

\linethickness does not affect the thickness of slanted lines, circles, or the quarter circles drawn by \oval.

8.19.8 \thicklines

The \thicklines command is an alternate line thickness for horizontal and vertical lines in a picture environment; cf. Section 8.19.7 [\linethickness], page 52, and Section 8.19.9 [\thinlines], page 52.

8.19.9 \thinlines

The \thinlines command is the default line thickness for horizontal and vertical lines in a picture environment; cf. Section 8.19.7 [\linethickness], page 52, and Section 8.19.8 [\thicklines], page 52.

8.19.10 \multiput

Synopsis:

> \multiput(*x,y*)(*delta_x,delta_y*){*n*}{*obj*}

The \multiput command copies the object *obj* in a regular pattern across a picture. *obj* is first placed at position (x, y), then at $(x + \delta x, y + \delta y)$, and so on, n times.

8.19.11 \oval

Synopsis:

> \oval(*width,height*)[*portion*]

The \oval command produces a rectangle with rounded corners. The optional argument *portion* allows you to produce only half of the oval via the following:

t   selects the top half;

b   selects the bottom half;

r   selects the right half;

l   selects the left half.

It is also possible to produce only one quarter of the oval by setting *portion* to `tr`, `br`, `bl`, or `tl`.

The "corners" of the oval are made with quarter circles with a maximum radius of 20 pt, so large "ovals" will look more like boxes with rounded corners.

8.19.12 \put

Synopsis:

> `\put(xcoord,ycoord){ ... }`

The `\put` command places the material specified by the (mandatory) argument in braces at the given coordinate, (*xcoord,ycoord*).

8.19.13 \shortstack

Synopsis:

> `\shortstack[position]{...\\...\\...}`

The `\shortstack` command produces a stack of objects. The valid positions are:

r   Move the objects to the right of the stack.

l   Move the objects to the left of the stack

c   Move the objects to the centre of the stack (default)

Objects are separated with `\\`.

8.19.14 \vector

Synopsis:

> `\vector(xslope,yslope){length}`

The `\vector` command draws a line with an arrow of the specified length and slope. The *xslope* and *yslope* values must lie between -4 and $+4$, inclusive.

8.20 quotation and quote

Synopsis:

> `\begin{quotation}`
> *text*
> `\end{quotation}`

or

> `\begin{quote}`
> *text*
> `\end{quote}`

Include a quotation.

In both environments, margins are indented on both sides by `\leftmargin` and the text is justified at both. As with the main text, leaving a blank line produces a new paragraph.

To compare the two: in the `quotation` environment, paragraphs are indented by 1.5 em and the space between paragraphs is small, `0pt plus 1pt`. In the `quote` environment, paragraphs are not indented and there is vertical space between paragraphs (it is the rubber length `\parsep`). Thus, the `quotation` environment may be more suitable for documents where new paragraphs are marked by an indent rather than by a vertical separation. In addition, `quote` may be more suitable for a short quotation or a sequence of short quotations.

```
\begin{quotation}
\it Four score and seven years ago
  ... shall not perish from the earth.
\hspace{1em plus 1fill}---Abraham Lincoln
\end{quotation}
```

8.21 `tabbing`

Synopsis:

```
\begin{tabbing}
row1col1 \= row1col2 \= row1col3 \= row1col4 \\
row2col1 \>                 \> row2col3 \\
...
\end{tabbing}
```

The `tabbing` environment provides a way to align text in columns. It works by setting tab stops and tabbing to them much as was done on an ordinary typewriter. It is best suited for cases where the width of each column is constant and known in advance.

This environment can be broken across pages, unlike the `tabular` environment.

The following commands can be used inside a `tabbing` environment:

`\\` (tabbing)
: End a line.

`\=` (tabbing)
: Sets a tab stop at the current position.

`\>` (tabbing)
: Advances to the next tab stop.

`\<`
: Put following text to the left of the local margin (without changing the margin). Can only be used at the start of the line.

`\+`
: Moves the left margin of the next and all the following commands one tab stop to the right, beginning tabbed line if necessary.

`\-`
: Moves the left margin of the next and all the following commands one tab stop to the left, beginning tabbed line if necessary.

`\'` (tabbing)
: Moves everything that you have typed so far in the current column, i.e., everything from the most recent `\>`, `\<`, `\'`, `\\`, or `\kill` command, to the right of the previous column, flush against the current column's tab stop.

\\` (tabbing)

> Allows you to put text flush right against any tab stop, including tab stop 0. However, it can't move text to the right of the last column because there's no tab stop there. The \\` command moves all the text that follows it, up to the \\\\ or \end{tabbing} command that ends the line, to the right margin of the tabbing environment. There must be no \\> or \\' command between the \\` and the command that ends the line.

\a (tabbing)

> In a **tabbing** environment, the commands \\=, \\' and \\` do not produce accents as usual (see Section 21.5 [Accents], page 118). Instead, the commands \a=, \a' and \a` are used.

\kill   Sets tab stops without producing text. Works just like \\\\ except that it throws away the current line instead of producing output for it. The effect of any \\=, \\+ or \\- commands in that line remain in effect.

\poptabs Restores the tab stop positions saved by the last \pushtabs.

\pushtabs

> Saves all current tab stop positions. Useful for temporarily changing tab stop positions in the middle of a **tabbing** environment.

\tabbingsep

> Distance to left of tab stop moved by \\'.

This example typesets a Pascal function in a traditional format:

```
\begin{tabbing}
function \= fact(n : integer) : integer;\\
        \> begin \= \+ \\
            \> if \= n $>$ 1 then \+ \\
                    fact := n * fact(n-1) \- \\
                else \+ \\
                    fact := 1; \-\- \\
            end;\\
\end{tabbing}
```

8.22 `table`

Synopsis:

```
\begin{table}[placement]
  table body
\caption[loftitle]{title}
\label{label}
\end{table}
```

A class of floats (see Section 5.6 [Floats], page 27). Because they cannot be split across pages, they are not typeset in sequence with the normal text but instead are "floated" to a convenient place, such as the top of a following page.

For the possible values of *placement* and their effect on the float placement algorithm, see Section 5.6 [Floats], page 27.

The table body is typeset in a `parbox` of width `\textwidth` and so it can contain text, commands, etc.

The label is optional; it is used for cross references (see Chapter 7 [Cross references], page 35). The optional `\caption` command specifies caption text for the table. By default it is numbered. If *lottitle* is present, it is used in the list of tables instead of *title* (see Section 23.1 [Tables of contents], page 122).

In this example the table and caption will float to the bottom of a page, unless it is pushed to a float page at the end.

```
\begin{table}[b]
  \centering
  \begin{tabular}{r|p{2in}} \hline
    One &The loneliest number \\
    Two &Can be as sad as one.
          It's the loneliest number since the number one.
  \end{tabular}
  \caption{Cardinal virtues}
  \label{tab:CardinalVirtues}
\end{table}
```

8.23 tabular

Synopsis:

```
\begin{tabular}[pos]{cols}
column 1 entry &column 2 entry ... &column n entry \\
   ...
\end{tabular}
```

or

```
\begin{tabular*}{width}[pos]{cols}
column 1 entry &column 2 entry ... &column n entry \\
   ...
\end{tabular*}
```

These environments produce a table, a box consisting of a sequence of horizontal rows. Each row consists of items that are aligned vertically in columns. This illustrates many of the features.

```
\begin{tabular}{l|l}
  \textit{Player name}  &\textit{Career home runs}  \\
  \hline
  Hank Aaron  &755 \\
  Babe Ruth   &714
\end{tabular}
```

The vertical format of two left-aligned columns, with a vertical bar between them, is specified in `tabular`'s argument `{l|l}`. Columns are separated with an ampersand `&`. A horizontal rule between two rows is created with `\hline`. The end of each row is marked with a double backslash `\\`. This `\\` is optional after the last row unless an `\hline` command follows, to put a rule below the table.

The required and optional arguments to `tabular` consist of:

width Required for `tabular*`, not allowed for `tabular`. Specifies the width of the `tabular*` environment. The space between columns should be rubber, as with `@{\extracolsep{\fill}}`, to allow the table to stretch or shrink to make the specified width, or else you are likely to get the `Underfull \hbox (badness 10000) in alignment` ... warning.

pos Optional. Specifies the table's vertical position. The default is to align the table so its vertical center matches the baseline of the surrounding text. There are two other possible alignments: `t` aligns the table so its top row matches the baseline of the surrounding text, and `b` aligns on the bottom row.

This only has an effect if there is other text. In the common case of a `tabular` alone in a `center` environment this option makes no difference.

cols Required. Specifies the formatting of columns. It consists of a sequence of the following specifiers, corresponding to the types of column and intercolumn material.

    `l`   A column of left-aligned items.

    `r`   A column of right-aligned items.

    `c`   A column of centered items.

    `|`   A vertical line the full height and depth of the environment.

`@{`*text or space*`}`

    This inserts *text or space* at this location in every row. The *text or space* material is typeset in LR mode. This text is fragile (see Section 12.9 [\protect], page 78).

    This specifier is optional: with no @-expression, LaTeX's `book`, `article`, and `report` classes will put on either side of each column a space of length `\tabcolsep`, which by default is '6pt'. That is, by default adjacent columns are separated by 12pt (so `\tabcolsep` is misleadingly-named since it is not the separation between tabular columns). By implication, a space of 6pt also comes before the first column and after the final column, unless you put a `@{...}` or `|` there.

    If you override the default and use an @-expression then you must insert any desired space yourself, as in `@{\hspace{1em}}`.

    An empty expression `@{}` will eliminate the space, including the space at the start or end, as in the example below where the tabular lines need to lie on the left margin.

```
\begin{flushleft}
  \begin{tabular}{@{}l}
    ...
  \end{tabular}
\end{flushleft}
```

This example shows text, a decimal point, between the columns, arranged so the numbers in the table are aligned on that decimal point.

```
\begin{tabular}{r@{$.$}l}
  $3$ &$14$  \\
  $9$ &$80665$
\end{tabular}
```

An `\extracolsep{wd}` command in an @-expression causes an extra space of width *wd* to appear to the left of all subsequent columns, until countermanded by another `\extracolsep` command. Unlike ordinary intercolumn space, this extra space is not suppressed by an @-expression. An `\extracolsep` command can be used only in an @-expression in the `cols` argument. Below, LaTeX inserts the right amount of intercolumn space to make the entire table 4 inches wide.

```
\begin{center}
  \begin{tabular*}{4in}{l@{\ \ldots\extracolsep{\fill}}l}
    Seven times down, eight times up
    &such is life!
  \end{tabular*}
\end{center}
```

To insert commands that are automatically executed before a given column, load the `array` package and use the `>{...}` specifier.

p{*wd*}   Each item in the column is typeset in a parbox of width *wd*.

Note that a line break double backslash `\\` may not appear in the item, except inside an environment like `minipage`, `array`, or `tabular`, or inside an explicit `\parbox`, or in the scope of a `\centering`, `\raggedright`, or `\raggedleft` declaration (when used in a p-column element these declarations must appear inside braces, as with `{\centering .. \\ ..}`). Otherwise LaTeX will misinterpret the double backslash as ending the row.

*{*num*}{*cols*}

Equivalent to *num* copies of *cols*, where *num* is a positive integer and *cols* is a list of specifiers. Thus `\begin{tabular}{|*{3}{l|r}|}` is equivalent to `\begin{tabular}{|l|rl|rl|r|}`. Note that *cols* may contain another *-expression.

Parameters that control formatting:

`\arrayrulewidth`

A length that is the thickness of the rule created by `|`, `\hline`, and `\vline` in the `tabular` and `array` environments. The default is '.4pt'. Change it as in `\setlength{\arrayrulewidth}{0.8pt}`.

`\arraystretch`

> A factor by which the spacing between rows in the **tabular** and **array** environments is multiplied. The default is '1', for no scaling. Change it as `\renewcommand{\arraystretch}{1.2}`.

`\doublerulesep`

> A length that is the distance between the vertical rules produced by the || specifier. The default is '2pt'.

`\tabcolsep`

> A length that is half of the space between columns. The default is '6pt'. Change it with `\setlength`.

The following commands can be used inside the body of a **tabular** environment, the first two inside an entry and the second two between lines:

8.23.1 `\multicolumn`

Synopsis:

```
\multicolumn{numcols}{cols}{text}
```

Make an **array** or **tabular** entry that spans several columns. The first argument *numcols* gives the number of columns to span. The second argument *cols* specifies the formatting of the entry, with c for centered, l for flush left, or r for flush right. The third argument *text* gives the contents of that entry.

In this example, in the first row, the second and third columns are spanned by the single heading 'Name'.

```
\begin{tabular}{lccl}
  \textit{ID}         &\multicolumn{2}{c}{\textit{Name}} &\textit{Age} \\ \hline % row one
  978-0-393-03701-2 &O'Brian &Patrick                    &55           \\         % row two
    ...
\end{tabular}
```

What counts as a column is: the column format specifier for the **array** or **tabular** environment is broken into parts, where each part (except the first) begins with l, c, r, or p. So from `\begin{tabular}{|r|ccp{1.5in}|}` the parts are |r|, c, c, and p{1.5in}|.

The *cols* argument overrides the **array** or **tabular** environment's intercolumn area default adjoining this multicolumn entry. To affect that area, this argument can contain vertical bars | indicating the placement of vertical rules, and @{...} expressions. Thus if *cols* is '|c|' then this multicolumn entry will be centered and a vertical rule will come in the intercolumn area before it and after it. This table details the exact behavior.

```
\begin{tabular}{|cc|c|c|}
  \multicolumn{1}{r}{w}       % entry one
    &\multicolumn{1}{|r|}{x}  % entry two
    &\multicolumn{1}{|r}{y}   % entry three
    &z                        % entry four
\end{tabular}
```

Before the first entry the output will not have a vertical rule because the `\multicolumn` has the *cols* specifier 'r' with no initial vertical bar. Between entry one and entry two there will be a vertical rule; although the first *cols* does not have an ending vertical bar, the second *cols* does have a starting one. Between entry two and entry three there is a single vertical rule; despite that the *cols* in both of the surrounding `multicolumn`'s call for a vertical rule, you only get one rule. Between entry three and entry four there is no vertical rule; the default calls for one but the *cols* in the entry three `\multicolumn` leaves it out, and that takes precedence. Finally, following entry four there is a vertical rule because of the default.

The number of spanned columns *numcols* can be 1. Besides giving the ability to change the horizontal alignment, this also is useful to override for one row the `tabular` definition's default intercolumn area specification, including the placement of vertical rules.

In the example below, in the `tabular` definition the first column is specified to default to left justified but in the first row the entry is centered with `\multicolumn{1}{c}{\textsc{Period}}`. Also in the first row, the second and third columns are spanned by a single entry with `\multicolumn{2}{c}{\textsc{Span}}`, overriding the specification to center those two columns on the page range en-dash.

```
\begin{tabular}{l|r@{--}l}
  \multicolumn{1}{c}{\textsc{Period}}
    &multicolumn{2}{c}{\textsc{Span}} \\ \hline
  Baroque          &1600          &1760          \\
  Classical        &1730          &1820          \\
  Romantic         &1780          &1910          \\
  Impressionistic  &1875          &1925
\end{tabular}
```

Note that although the `tabular` specification by default puts a vertical rule between the first and second columns, because there is no vertical bar in the *cols* of either of the first row's `\multicolumn` commands, no rule appears in the first row.

8.23.2 `\vline`

Draw a vertical line in a `tabular` or `array` environment extending the full height and depth of an entry's row. Can also be used in an @-expression, although its synonym vertical bar | is more common. This command is rarely used in the body of a table; typically a table's vertical lines are specified in `tabular`'s *cols* argument and overridden as needed with `\multicolumn`.

This example illustrates some pitfalls. In the first line's second entry the `\hfill` moves the `\vline` to the left edge of the cell. But that is different than putting it halfway between the two columns, so in that row between the first and second columns there are two vertical rules, with the one from the `{c|cc}` specifier coming before the one produced by the `\vline\hfill`. In contrast, the first line's third entry shows the usual way to put a vertical bar between two columns. In the second line, the `ghi` is the widest entry in its column so in the `\vline\hfill` the `\hfill` has no effect and the vertical line in that entry appears immediately next to the g, with no whitespace.

```
\begin{tabular}{c|cc}
  x   &\vline\hfill y   &\multicolumn{1}{|r}{z} \\
  abc &def &\vline\hfill ghi
\end{tabular}
```

8.23.3 \cline

Synopsis:

> \cline{*i-j*}

Draw a horizontal rule in an **array** or **tabular** environment beginning in column *i* and ending in column *j*. The dash – must appear in the mandatory argument. To span a single column use the number twice.

This example puts two horizontal lines between the first and second rows, one line in the first column only, and the other spanning the third and fourth columns. The two lines are side-by-side, at the same height.

```
\begin{tabular}{llrr}
  a &b &c &d \\ \cline{1-1} \cline{3-4}
  e &f &g &h
\end{tabular}
```

8.23.4 \hline

Draws a horizontal line the width of the enclosing **tabular** or **array** environment. It's most commonly used to draw a line at the top, bottom, and between the rows of a table.

In this example the top of the table has two horizontal rules, one above the other, that span both columns. The bottom of the table has a single rule spanning both columns. Because of the \hline, the **tabular** second row's line ending double backslash \\ is required.

```
\begin{tabular}{ll} \hline\hline
  Baseball   &Red Sox  \\
  Basketball &Celtics  \\ \hline
\end{tabular}
```

8.24 thebibliography

Synopsis:

> \begin{thebibliography}{*widest-label*}
> \bibitem[*label*]{*cite_key*}
>
> ...
>
> \end{thebibliography}

The **thebibliography** environment produces a bibliography or reference list.

In the **article** class, this reference list is labelled "References"; in the **report** class, it is labelled "Bibliography". You can change the label (in the standard classes) by redefining the command **\refname**. For instance, this eliminates it entirely:

> \renewcommand{\refname}{}

The mandatory *widest-label* argument is text that, when typeset, is as wide as the widest item label produced by the **\bibitem** commands. It is typically given as **9** for bibliographies with less than 10 references, **99** for ones with less than 100, etc.

8.24.1 \bibitem

Synopsis:

> \bibitem[*label*]{*cite_key*}

The \bibitem command generates an entry labelled by *label*. If the *label* argument is missing, a number is automatically generated using the **enumi** counter. The *cite_key* is a *citation key* consisting in any sequence of letters, numbers, and punctuation symbols not containing a comma.

This command writes an entry to the .aux file containing the item's *cite_key* and *label*. When the .aux file is read by the \begin{document} command, the item's *label* is associated with cite_key, causing references to *cite_key* with a \cite command (see Section 8.24.2 [\cite], page 62) to produce the associated *label*.

8.24.2 \cite

Synopsis:

> \cite[*subcite*]{*keys*}

The *keys* argument is a list of one or more citation keys (see Section 8.24.1 [\bibitem], page 61), separated by commas. This command generates an in-text citation to the references associated with *keys* by entries in the .aux file.

The text of the optional *subcite* argument appears after the citation. For example, \cite[p.~314]{knuth} might produce '[Knuth, p. 314]'.

8.24.3 \nocite

Synopsis:

> \nocite{*keys*}

The \nocite command produces no text, but writes *keys*, which is a list of one or more citation keys, to the .aux file.

8.24.4 Using BibTeX

If you use the BibTeX program by Oren Patashnik (highly recommended if you need a bibliography of more than a couple of titles) to maintain your bibliography, you don't use the **thebibliography** environment (see Section 8.24 [thebibliography], page 61). Instead, you include the lines

> \bibliographystyle{*bibstyle*}
> \bibliography{*bibfile1,bibfile2*}

The \bibliographystyle command does not produce any output of its own. Rather, it defines the style in which the bibliography will be produced: *bibstyle* refers to a file *bibstyle*.bst, which defines how your citations will look. The standard *bibstyle* names distributed with BibTeX are:

alpha   Sorted alphabetically. Labels are formed from name of author and year of publication.

plain   Sorted alphabetically. Labels are numeric.

unsrt   Like **plain**, but entries are in order of citation.

abbrv   Like **plain**, but more compact labels.

In addition, numerous other BibTeX style files exist tailored to the demands of various publications. See http://mirror.ctan.org/biblio/bibtex/contrib.

The `\bibliography` command is what actually produces the bibliography. The argument to `\bibliography` refers to files named *bibfile1*`.bib`, *bibfile2*`.bib`, ..., which should contain your database in BibTeX format. Only the entries referred to via `\cite` and `\nocite` will be listed in the bibliography.

8.25 `theorem`

Synopsis:

```
\begin{theorem}
theorem-text
\end{theorem}
```

The `theorem` environment produces "Theorem *n*" in boldface followed by *theorem-text*, where the numbering possibilities for *n* are described under `\newtheorem` (see Section 12.7 [\newtheorem], page 76).

8.26 `titlepage`

Synopsis:

```
\begin{titlepage}
  ... text and spacing ...
\end{titlepage}
```

Create a title page, a page with no printed page number or heading. The following page will be numbered page one.

To instead produce a standard title page without a `titlepage` environment you can use `\maketitle` (see Section 18.1 [\maketitle], page 105).

Notice in this example that all formatting, including vertical spacing, is left to the author.

```
\begin{titlepage}
\vspace*{\stretch{1}}
\begin{center}
  {\huge\bfseries Thesis \\[1ex]
                  title}                    \\[6.5ex]
  {\large\bfseries Author name}             \\
  \vspace{4ex}
  Thesis  submitted to                      \\[5pt]
  \textit{University name}                   \\[2cm]
  in partial fulfilment for the award of the degree of \\[2cm]
  \textsc{\Large Doctor of Philosophy}      \\[2ex]
  \textsc{\large Mathematics}               \\[12ex]
  \vfill
  Department of Mathematics                 \\
  Address                                   \\
  \vfill
  \today
\end{center}
\vspace{\stretch{2}}
\end{titlepage}
```

8.27 `verbatim`

Synopsis:

```
\begin{verbatim}
literal-text
\end{verbatim}
```

The `verbatim` environment is a paragraph-making environment in which LaTeX produces exactly what you type in; for instance the \ character produces a printed '\'. It turns LaTeX into a typewriter with carriage returns and blanks having the same effect that they would on a typewriter.

The `verbatim` uses a monospaced typewriter-like font (`\tt`).

8.27.1 `\verb`

Synopsis:

```
\verbcharliteral-textchar
\verb*charliteral-textchar
```

The `\verb` command typesets *literal-text* as it is input, including special characters and spaces, using the typewriter (`\tt`) font. No spaces are allowed between `\verb` or `\verb*` and the delimiter *char*, which begins and ends the verbatim text. The delimiter must not appear in *literal-text*.

The `*`-form differs only in that spaces are printed with a "visible space" character. (Namely, ␣.)

8.28 `verse`

Synopsis:

```
\begin{verse}
line1 \\
line2 \\
...
\end{verse}
```

The `verse` environment is designed for poetry, though you may find other uses for it.

The margins are indented on the left and the right, paragraphs are not indented, and the text is not justified. Separate the lines of each stanza with \\, and use one or more blank lines to separate the stanzas.

9 Line breaking

The first thing LaTeX does when processing ordinary text is to translate your input file into a sequence of glyphs and spaces. To produce a printed document, this sequence must be broken into lines (and these lines must be broken into pages).

LaTeX usually does the line (and page) breaking in the text body for you but in some environments you manually force line breaks.

9.1 \\

Synopsis:

> \\[*morespace*]

or

> *[*morespace*]

Start a new line. The optional argument *morespace* specifies extra vertical space to be insert before the next line. This can be a negative length. The text before the break is set at its normal length, that is, it is not stretched to fill out the line width.

Explicit line breaks in the text body are unusual in LaTeX. In particular, to start a new paragraph instead leave a blank line. This command is mostly used outside of the main flow of text such as in a tabular or array environment.

Under ordinary circumstances (e.g., outside of a p{...} column in a tabular environment) the \newline command is a synonym for \\ (see Section 9.3 [\newline], page 65).

In addition to starting a new line, the starred form * tells LaTeX not to start a new page between the two lines, by issuing a \nobreak.

```
\title{My story: \\[0.25in]
        a tale of woe}
```

9.2 \obeycr & \restorecr

The \obeycr command makes a return in the input file (`^^M`, internally) the same as \\ (followed by \relax). So each new line in the input will also be a new line in the output.

\restorecr restores normal line-breaking behavior.

9.3 \newline

In ordinary text this is equivalent to double-backslash (see Section 9.1 [\\], page 65); it breaks a line, with no stretching of the text before it.

Inside a tabular or array environment, in a column with a specifier producing a paragraph box, like typically p{...}, \newline will insert a line break inside of the column, that is, it does not break the entire row. To break the entire row use \\ or its equivalent \tabularnewline.

This will print 'Name:' and 'Address:' as two lines in a single cell of the table.

```
\begin{tabular}{p{1in}{\hspace{2in}}p{1in}}
  Name: \newline Address: &Date: \\ \hline
\end{tabular}
```

The 'Date:' will be baseline-aligned with 'Name:'.

9.4 \- (discretionary hyphen)

The \- command tells LaTeX that it may hyphenate the word at that point. LaTeX is pretty good at hyphenating, and usually finds most of the correct hyphenation points, while almost never using an incorrect one. The \- command is used for the exceptional cases.

When you insert \- commands in a word, the word will only be hyphenated at those points and not at any of the hyphenation points that LaTeX might otherwise have chosen.

9.5 \discretionary (generalized hyphenation point)

Synopsis:

> \discretionary{*pre-break-text*}{*post-break-text*}{*no-break-text*}

9.6 \fussy

The declaration \fussy (which is the default) makes TeX picky about line breaking. This usually avoids too much space between words, at the cost of an occasional overfull box.

This command cancels the effect of a previous \sloppy command (see Section 9.7 [\sloppy], page 66).

9.7 \sloppy

The declaration \sloppy makes TeX less fussy about line breaking. This will avoid overfull boxes, at the cost of loose interword spacing.

Lasts until a \fussy command is issued (see Section 9.6 [\fussy], page 66).

9.8 \hyphenation

Synopsis:

> \hyphenation{*word-one word-two*}

The \hyphenation command declares allowed hyphenation points with a - character in the given words. The words are separated by spaces. TeX will only hyphenate if the word matches exactly, no inflections are tried. Multiple \hyphenation commands accumulate. Some examples (the default TeX hyphenation patterns misses the hyphenations in these words):

> \hyphenation{ap-pen-dix col-umns data-base data-bases}

9.9 \linebreak & \nolinebreak

Synopses:

> \linebreak[*priority*]
> \nolinebreak[*priority*]

By default, the \linebreak (\nolinebreak) command forces (prevents) a line break at the current position. For \linebreak, the spaces in the line are stretched out so that it extends to the right margin as usual.

With the optional argument *priority*, you can convert the command from a demand to a request. The *priority* must be a number from 0 to 4. The higher the number, the more insistent the request.

10 Page breaking

LaTeX starts new pages asynchronously, when enough material has accumulated to fill up a page. Usually this happens automatically, but sometimes you may want to influence the breaks.

10.1 \cleardoublepage

The \cleardoublepage command ends the current page and causes all the pending floating figures and tables that have so far appeared in the input to be printed. In a two-sided printing style, it also makes the next page a right-hand (odd-numbered) page, producing a blank page if necessary.

10.2 \clearpage

The \clearpage command ends the current page and causes all the pending floating figures and tables that have so far appeared in the input to be printed.

10.3 \newpage

The \newpage command ends the current page, but does not clear floats (see Section 10.2 [\clearpage], page 67).

10.4 \enlargethispage

\enlargethispage{size}

\enlargethispage*{size}

Enlarge the \textheight for the current page by the specified amount; e.g., \enlargethispage{\baselineskip} will allow one additional line.

The starred form tries to squeeze the material together on the page as much as possible. This is normally used together with an explicit \pagebreak.

10.5 \pagebreak & \nopagebreak

Synopses:

\pagebreak[*priority*]
\nopagebreak[*priority*]

By default, the \pagebreak (\nopagebreak) command forces (prevents) a page break at the current position. With \pagebreak, the vertical space on the page is stretched out where possible so that it extends to the normal bottom margin.

With the optional argument *priority*, you can convert the \pagebreak command from a demand to a request. The number must be a number from 0 to 4. The higher the number, the more insistent the request is.

11 Footnotes

Place a numbered footnote at the bottom of the current page, as here.

```
Noël Coward quipped that having to read a footnote is like having
to go downstairs to answer the door, while in the midst of making
love.\footnote{I wouldn't know, I don't read footnotes.}
```

You can place multiple footnotes on a page. If the text becomes too long it will flow to the next page.

You can also produce footnotes by combining the `\footnotemark` and the `\footnotetext` commands, which is useful in special circumstances.

To make bibliographic references come out as footnotes you need to include a bibliographic style with that behavior.

11.1 `\footnote`

Synopsis:

```
\footnote[number]{text}
```

Place a numbered footnote *text* at the bottom of the current page.

```
There are over a thousand footnotes in Gibbon's
\textit{Decline and Fall of the Roman Empire}.\footnote{After
reading an early version with endnotes David Hume complained,
''One is also plagued with his Notes, according to the present Method
of printing the Book'' and suggested that they ''only to be printed
at the Margin or the Bottom of the Page.''}
```

The optional argument *number* allows you to specify the footnote number. If you use this option then the footnote number counter is not incremented, and if you do not use it then the counter is incremented.

Change how LaTeX shows the footnote counter with something like `\renewcommand{\thefootnote}{\fnsymbol{footnote}}`, which uses a sequence of symbols (see Section 13.1 [\alph \Alph \arabic \roman \Roman \fnsymbol], page 80). To make this change global put that in the preamble. If you make the change local then you may want to reset the counter with `\setcounter{footnote}{0}`. By default LaTeX uses arabic numbers.

LaTeX's default puts many restrictions on where you can use a `\footnote`; for instance, you cannot use it in an argument to a sectioning command such as `\chapter` (it can only be used in outer paragraph mode). There are some workarounds; see following sections.

In a `minipage` environment the `\footnote` command uses the `mpfootnote` counter instead of the `footnote` counter, so they are numbered independently. They are shown at the bottom of the environment, not at the bottom of the page. And by default they are shown alphabetically. See Section 8.18 [minipage], page 49.

11.2 \footnotemark

Synopsis, one of:

```
\footnotemark
\footnotemark[number]
```

Put the current footnote number in the text. (See Section 11.3 [\footnotetext], page 69, for giving the text of the footnote separately.) The version with the optional argument *number* uses that number to determine the mark printed. This command can be used in inner paragraph mode.

This example gives the same institutional affiliation to both the first and third authors (\thanks is a version of footnote).

```
\title{A Treatise on the Binomial Theorem}
\author{J Moriarty\thanks{University of Leeds}
  \and A C Doyle\thanks{Durham University}
  \and S Holmes\footnotemark[1]}
\begin{document}
\maketitle
```

If you use \footnotemark without the optional argument then it increments the footnote counter but if you use the optional *number* then it does not. This produces several consecutive footnote markers referring to the same footnote.

```
The first theorem\footnote{Due to Gauss.}
and the second theorem\footnotemark[\value{footnote}]
and the third theorem.\footnotemark[\value{footnote}]
```

11.3 \footnotetext

Synopsis, one of:

```
\footnotetext{text}
\footnotetext[number]{text}
```

Place *text* at the bottom of the page as a footnote. This command can come anywhere after the \footnotemark command. The optional argument *number* changes the displayed footnote number. The \footnotetext command must appear in outer paragraph mode.

11.4 Footnotes in a table

Inside a table environment the \footnote command does not work. For instance, if the code below appears on its own then the footnote simply disappears; there is a footnote mark in the table cell but nothing is set at the bottom of the page.

```
\begin{center}
    \begin{tabular}{l|l}
    \textsc{Ship}  &\textsc{Book} \\ \hline
    \textit{HMS Sophie}     &Master and Commander  \\
    \textit{HMS Polychrest} &Post Captain  \\
    \textit{HMS Lively}     &Post Captain \\
    \textit{HMS Surprise}   &A number of books\footnote{Starting with
                             HMS Surprise.}
```

```
    \end{tabular}
  \end{center}
```

The solution is to surround the `tabular` environment with a `minipage` environment, as here (see Section 8.18 [minipage], page 49).

```
  \begin{center}
    \begin{minipage}{.5\textwidth}
      ... tabular material ...
    \end{minipage}
  \end{center}
```

The same technique will work inside a floating `table` environment (see Section 8.22 [table], page 55). To get the footnote at the bottom of the page use the `tablefootnote` package, as illustrated in this example. If you put `\usepackage{tablefootnote}` in the preamble and use the code shown then the footnote appears at the bottom and is numbered in sequence with other footnotes.

```
  \begin{table}
    \centering
      \begin{tabular}{l|l}
      \textsc{Date}  &\textsc{Campaign} \\ \hline
      1862            &Fort Donelson \\
      1863            &Vicksburg     \\
      1865            &Army of Northern Virginia\footnote{Ending the war.}
      \end{tabular}
    \caption{Forces captured by US Grant}
  \end{table}
```

11.5 Footnotes in section headings

Putting a footnote in a section heading, as in:

```
  \section{Full sets\protect\footnote{This material due to ...}}
```

causes the footnote to appear at the bottom of the page where the section starts, as usual, but also at the bottom of the table of contents, where it is not likely to be desired. To have it not appear on the table of contents use the package `footmisc` with the `stable` option.

```
  \usepackage[stable]{footmisc}
  ...
  \begin{document}
  ...
  \section{Full sets\footnote{This material due to ...}}
```

Note that the `\protect` is gone; including it would cause the footnote to reappear on the table of contents.

11.6 Footnotes of footnotes

Particularly in the humanities, authors can have multiple classes of footnotes, including having footnotes of footnotes. The package `bigfoot` extends LaTeX's default footnote mechanism in many ways, including allow these two, as in this example.

```
  \usepackage{bigfoot}
```

```
\DeclareNewFootnote{Default}
\DeclareNewFootnote{from}[alph]   % create class \footnotefrom{}
  ...
\begin{document}
...
The third theorem is a partial converse of the
second.\footnotefrom{First noted in Wilson.\footnote{Second edition only.}}
...
```

11.7 Multiple references to footnotes

You can refer to a single footnote more than once. This example uses the package cleverref.

```
\usepackage{cleveref}[2012/02/15]   % this version of package or later
\crefformat{footnote}{#2\footnotemark[#1]#3}
  ...
\begin{document}
...
The theorem is from Evers.\footnote{\label{fn:TE}Tinker and Evers, 1994.}
The corollary is from Chance.\footnote{Evers and Chance, 1990.}
But the key lemma is from Tinker.\cref{fn:TE}
...
```

This solution will work with the package hyperref. See Section 11.2 [\footnotemark], page 69, for a simpler solution in the common case of multiple authors with the same affiliation.

11.8 Footnote parameters

\footnoterule

> Produces the rule separating the main text on a page from the page's footnotes. Default dimensions: 0.4pt thick (or wide), and 0.4\columnwidth long in the standard document classes (except slides, where it does not appear).

\footnotesep

> The height of the strut placed at the beginning of the footnote. By default, this is set to the normal strut for \footnotesize fonts (see Section 4.2 [Font sizes], page 19), therefore there is no extra space between footnotes. This is '6.65pt' for '10pt', '7.7pt' for '11pt', and '8.4pt' for '12pt'.

12 Definitions

LaTeX has support for making new commands of many different kinds.

12.1 \newcommand & \renewcommand

\newcommand and \renewcommand define and redefine a command, respectively. Synopses:

```
\newcommand{\cmd}[nargs][optargdefault]{defn}
\newcommand*{\cmd}[nargs][optargdefault]{defn}
\renewcommand{\cmd}[nargs][optargdefault]{defn}
\renewcommand*{\cmd}[nargs][optargdefault]{defn}
```

The starred form of these two commands requires that the arguments not contain multiple paragraphs of text (not \long, in plain TeX terms).

cmd   Required; \cmd is the command name. For \newcommand, it must not be already defined and must not begin with \end. For \renewcommand, it must already be defined.

nargs   Optional; an integer from 0 to 9, specifying the number of arguments that the command can take, including any optional argument. If this argument is not present, the default is for the command to have no arguments. When redefining a command, the new version can have a different number of arguments than the old version.

optargdefault

Optional; if this argument is present then the first argument of defined command \cmd is optional, with default value *optargdefault* (which may be the empty string). If this argument is not present then \cmd does not take an optional argument.

That is, if \cmd is used with square brackets following, as in \cmd[myval], then within *defn* the first *positional parameter* #1 expands *myval*. On the other hand, if \cmd is called without square brackets following, then within *defn* the positional parameter #1 expands to the default *optargdefault*. In either case, any required arguments will be referred to starting with #2.

Omitting [myval] in a call is different from having the square brackets with no contents, as in []. The former results in #1 expanding to *optargdefault*; the latter results in #1 expanding to the empty string.

defn   The text to be substituted for every occurrence of \cmd; the positional parameter #n in *defn* is replaced by the text of the *n*th argument.

TeX ignores spaces in the source following an alphabetic control sequence, as in '\cmd '. If you actually want a space there, one solution is to type {} after the command ('\cmd{} '; another solution is to use an explicit control space ('\cmd\ ').

A simple example of defining a new command: \newcommand{\RS}{Robin Smith} results in \RS being replaced by the longer text.

Redefining an existing command is similar: \renewcommand{\qedsymbol}{{\small QED}}.

Here's a command definition with one required argument:

```
\newcommand{\defref}[1]{Definition~\ref{#1}}
```

Then, `\defref{def:basis}` expands to `Definition~\ref{def:basis}`, which will ultimately expand to something like 'Definition~3.14'.

An example with two required arguments: `\newcommand{\nbym}[2]{$#1 \times #2$}` is invoked as `\nbym{2}{k}`.

An example with an optional argument:

```
\newcommand{\salutation}[1][Sir or Madam]{Dear #1:}
```

Then, `\salutation` gives 'Dear Sir or Madam:' while `\salutation[John]` gives 'Dear John:'. And `\salutation[]` gives 'Dear :'.

The braces around *defn* do not define a group, that is, they do not delimit the scope of the result of expanding *defn*. So `\newcommand{\shipname}[1]{\it #1}` is problematic; in this sentence,

```
The \shipname{Monitor} met the \shipname{Merrimac}.
```

the words 'met the' would incorrectly be in italics. Another pair of braces in the definition is needed, like this: `\newcommand{\shipname}[1]{{\it #1}}`. Those braces are part of the definition and thus do define a group.

12.2 \providecommand

Defines a command, as long as no command of this name already exists. Synopses:

```
\providecommand{cmd}[nargs][optargdefault]{defn}
\providecommand*{cmd}[nargs][optargdefault]{defn}
```

If no command of this name already exists then this has the same effect as `\newcommand` (see Section 12.1 [\newcommand & \renewcommand], page 72). If a command of this name already exists then this definition does nothing. This is particularly useful in a style file, or other file that may be loaded more than once.

12.3 \newcounter: Allocating a counter

Synopsis, one of:

```
\newcounter{countername}
\newcounter{countername}[supercounter]
```

Globally defines a new counter named *countername* and initialize the new counter to zero.

The name *countername* must consists of letters only, and does not begin with a backslash. This name must not already be in use by another counter.

When you use the optional argument [*supercounter*] then *countername* will be numbered within, or subsidiary to, the existing counter *supercounter*. For example, ordinarily `subsection` is numbered within `section` so that any time *supercounter* is incremented with `\stepcounter` (see Section 13.7 [\stepcounter], page 82) or `\refstepcounter` (see Section 13.6 [\refstepcounter], page 82) then *countername* is reset to zero.

See Chapter 13 [Counters], page 80, for more information about counters.

12.4 \newlength: Allocating a length

Allocate a new *length* register. Synopsis:

> \newlength{\arg}

This command takes one required argument, which must begin with a backslash ('\'). It creates a new length register named \arg, which is a place to hold (rubber) lengths such as 1in plus.2in minus.1in (what plain TeX calls a skip register). The register gets an initial value of zero. The control sequence \arg must not already be defined.

See Chapter 14 [Lengths], page 83, for more about lengths.

12.5 \newsavebox: Allocating a box

Allocate a "bin" for holding a box. Synopsis:

> \newsavebox{\cmd}

Defines \cmd to refer to a new bin for storing boxes. Such a box is for holding typeset material, to use multiple times (see Chapter 20 [Boxes], page 111) or to measure or manipulate. The name \cmd must start with a backslash ('\'), and must not be already defined.

The allocation of a box is global. This command is fragile (see Section 12.9 [\protect], page 78).

12.6 \newenvironment & \renewenvironment

These commands define or redefine an environment *env*, that is, \begin{env} *body* \end{env}. Synopses:

> \newenvironment{*env*}[*nargs*] [*optargdefault*]{*begdefn*}{*enddefn*}
> \newenvironment*{*env*}[*nargs*] [*optargdefault*]{*begdefn*}{*enddefn*}
> \renewenvironment{*env*}[*nargs*] [*optargdefault*]{*begdefn*}{*enddefn*}
> \renewenvironment*{*env*}[*nargs*] [*optargdefault*]{*begdefn*}{*enddefn*}

The starred form of these commands requires that the arguments not contain multiple paragraphs of text. The body of these environments can still contain multiple paragraphs.

env   Required; the environment name. It consists only of letters or the * character, and thus does not begin with backslash (\). It must not begin with the string end. For \newenvironment, the name *env* must not be the name of an already existing environment, and also the command \env must be undefined. For \renewenvironment, *env* must be the name of an existing environment.

nargs   Optional; an integer from 0 to 9 denoting the number of arguments of that the environment will take. When the environment is used these arguments appear after the \begin, as in \begin{env}{arg1}...{argn}. If this argument is not present then the default is for the environment to have no arguments. When redefining an environment, the new version can have a different number of arguments than the old version.

optargdefault

     Optional; if this argument is present then the first argument of the defined environment is optional, with default value *optargdefault* (which may be the empty string). If this argument is not present then the environment does not take an optional argument.

That is, when `[optargdefault]` is present in the environment definition, if `\begin{env}` is used with square brackets following, as in `\begin{env}[myval]`, then, within *begdefn*, the positional parameter `#1` expands to *myval*. If `\begin{env}` is called without square brackets following, then, within within *begdefn*, the positional parameter `#1` expands to the default *optargdefault*. In either case, any required arguments will be referred to starting with `#2`.

Omitting `[myval]` in the call is different from having the square brackets with no contents, as in `[]`. The former results in `#1` expanding to *optargdefault*; the latter results in `#1` expanding to the empty string.

begdefn   Required; the text expanded at every occurrence of `\begin{env}`. Within *begdef*, the *n*th positional parameter (i.e., `#n`) is replaced by the text of the *n*th argument.

enddefn   Required; the text expanded at every occurrence of `\end{env}`. This may not contain any positional parameters, so `#n` cannot be used here (but see the final example below).

All environments, that is to say the *begdefn* code, the environment body and the *enddefn* code, are processed within a group. Thus, in the first example below, the effect of the `\small` is limited to the quote and does not extend to material following the environment.

This example gives an environment like LaTeX's `quotation` except that it will be set in smaller type:

```
\newenvironment{smallquote}{%
  \small\begin{quotation}
}{%
  \end{quotation}
}
```

This one shows the use of arguments; it gives a quotation environment that cites the author:

```
\newenvironment{citequote}[1][Shakespeare]{%
  \begin{quotation}
  \noindent\textit{#1}:
}{%
  \end{quotation}
}
```

The author's name is optional, and defaults to 'Shakespeare'. In the document, use the environment like this:

```
\begin{citequote}[Lincoln]
  ...
\end{citequote}
```

The final example shows how to save the value of an argument to use in *enddefn*, in this case in a box (see Section 20.8 [\sbox], page 113):

```
\newsavebox{\quoteauthor}
```

```
\newenvironment{citequote}[1][Shakespeare]{%
  \sbox\quoteauthor{#1}%
  \begin{quotation}
}{%
  \hspace{1em plus 1fill}---\usebox{\quoteauthor}
  \end{quotation}
}
```

12.7 \newtheorem

Define a new theorem-like environment. Synopses:

```
\newtheorem{name}{title}
\newtheorem{name}{title}[numbered_within]
\newtheorem{name}[numbered_like]{title}
```

Using the first form, `\newtheorem{name}{title}` creates an environment that will be labelled with *title*. See the first example below.

The second form `\newtheorem{name}{title}[numbered_within]` creates an environment whose counter is subordinate to the existing counter *numbered_within* (its counter will be reset when *numbered_within* is reset).

The third form `\newtheorem{name}[numbered_like]{title}`, with optional argument between the two required arguments, will create an environment whose counter will share the previously defined counter *numbered_like*.

You can specify one of *numbered_within* and *numbered_like*, or neither, but not both.

This command creates a counter named *name*. In addition, unless the optional argument *numbered_like* is used, inside of the theorem-like environment the current `\ref` value will be that of `\thenumbered_within` (see Section 7.3 [\ref], page 36).

This declaration is global. It is fragile (see Section 12.9 [\protect], page 78).

Arguments:

name   The name of the environment. It must not begin with a backslash ('\'). It must not be the name of an existing environment; indeed, the command name `\name` must not already be defined as anything.

title   The text printed at the beginning of the environment, before the number. For example, 'Theorem'.

numbered_within

Optional; the name of an already defined counter, usually a sectional unit such as `chapter` or `section`. When the *numbered_within* counter is reset then the *name* environment's counter will also be reset.

If this optional argument is not used then the command `\thename` is set to `\arabic{name}`.

numbered_like

Optional; the name of an already defined theorem-like environment. The new environment will be numbered in sequence with *numbered_like*.

Without any optional arguments the environments are numbered sequentially. The example below has a declaration in the preamble that results in 'Definition 1' and 'Definition 2' in the output.

```
\newtheorem{defn}{Definition}
\begin{document}
\section{...}
\begin{defn}
  First def
\end{defn}

\section{...}
\begin{defn}
  Second def
\end{defn}
```

Because the next example specifies the optional argument *numbered_within* to \newtheorem as section, the example, with the same document body, gives 'Definition 1.1' and 'Definition 2.1'.

```
\newtheorem{defn}{Definition}[section]
\begin{document}
\section{...}
\begin{defn}
  First def
\end{defn}

\section{...}
\begin{defn}
  Second def
\end{defn}
```

In the next example there are two declarations in the preamble, the second of which calls for the new thm environment to use the same counter as defn. It gives 'Definition 1.1', followed by 'Theorem 2.1' and 'Definition 2.2'.

```
\newtheorem{defn}{Definition}[section]
\newtheorem{thm}[defn]{Theorem}
\begin{document}
\section{...}
\begin{defn}
  First def
\end{defn}

\section{...}
\begin{thm}
  First thm
\end{thm}

\begin{defn}
  Second def
```

```
\end{defn}
```

12.8 \newfont: Define a new font (obsolete)

\newfont, now obsolete, defines a command that will switch fonts. Synopsis:

```
\newfont{\cmd}{font description}
```

This defines a control sequence \cmd that will change the current font. LaTeX will look on your system for a file named *fontname*.tfm. The control sequence must must not already be defined. It must begin with a backslash ('\').

This command is obsolete. It is a low-level command for setting up an individual font. Today fonts are almost always defined in families (which allows you to, for example, associate a boldface with a roman) through the so-called "New Font Selection Scheme", either by using .fd files or through the use of an engine that can access system fonts such as XeLaTeX (see Section 2.3 [TeX engines], page 4).

But since it is part of LaTeX, here is an explanation: the *font description* consists of a *fontname* and an optional *at clause*; this can have the form either **at dimen** or **scaled factor**, where a *factor* of '1000' means no scaling. For LaTeX's purposes, all this does is scale all the character and other font dimensions relative to the font's design size, which is a value defined in the .tfm file.

This example defines two equivalent fonts and typesets a few characters in each:

```
\newfont{\testfontat}{cmb10 at 11pt}
\newfont{\testfontscaled}{cmb10 scaled 1100}
\testfontat abc
\testfontscaled abc
```

12.9 \protect

All LaTeX commands are either *fragile* or *robust*. A fragile command can break when it is used in the argument to certain other commands. Commands that contain data that LaTeX writes to an auxiliary file and re-reads later are fragile. This includes material that goes into a table of contents, list of figures, list of tables, etc. Fragile commands also include line breaks, any command that has an optional argument, and many more. To prevent such commands from breaking, one solution is to preceded them with the command \protect.

For example, when LaTeX runs the \section{section name} command it writes the *section name* text to the .aux auxiliary file, moving it there for use elsewhere in the document such as in the table of contents. Any argument that is internally expanded by LaTeX without typesetting it directly is referred to as a *moving argument*. A command is fragile if it can expand during this process into invalid TeX code. Some examples of moving arguments are those that appear in the \caption{...} command (see Section 8.10 [figure], page 44), in the \thanks{...} command (see Section 18.1 [\maketitle], page 105), and in @-expressions in the **tabular** and **array** environments (see Section 8.23 [tabular], page 56).

If you get strange errors from commands used in moving arguments, try preceding it with \protect. Every fragile commands must be protected with their own \protect.

Although usually a \protect command doesn't hurt, length commands are robust and should not be preceded by a \protect command. Nor can a \protect command be used in the argument to \addtocounter or \setcounter command.

In this example the `\caption` command gives a mysterious error about an extra curly brace. Fix the problem by preceding each `\raisebox` command with `\protect`.

```
\begin{figure}
   ...
   \caption{Company headquarters of A\raisebox{1pt}{B}\raisebox{-1pt}{C}}
\end{figure}
```

In the next example the `\tableofcontents` command gives an error because the `\(..\)` in the section title expands to illegal TeX in the `.toc` file. You can solve this by changing `\(..\)` to `\protect\(..\protect\)`.

```
\begin{document}
\tableofcontents
...
\section{Einstein's \( e=mc^2 \)}
...
```

13 Counters

Everything LATEX numbers for you has a counter associated with it. The name of the counter is often the same as the name of the environment or command associated with the number, except that the counter's name has no backslash \. Thus, associated with the \chapter command is the chapter counter that keeps track of the chapter number.

Below is a list of the counters used in LATEX's standard document classes to control numbering.

part	paragraph	figure	enumi
chapter	subparagraph	table	enumii
section	page	footnote	enumiii
subsection	equation	mpfootnote	enumiv
subsubsection			

The mpfootnote counter is used by the \footnote command inside of a minipage (see Section 8.18 [minipage], page 49). The counters enumi through enumiv are used in the enumerate environment, for up to four levels of nesting (see Section 8.7 [enumerate], page 42).

New counters are created with \newcounter. See Section 12.3 [\newcounter], page 73.

13.1 \alph \Alph \arabic \roman \Roman \fnsymbol: Printing counters

Print the value of a counter, in a specified style. For instance, if the counter *counter* has the value 1 then a \alph{*counter*} in your source will result in a lower case letter a appearing in the output.

All of these commands take a single counter as an argument, for instance, \alph{enumi}. Note that the counter name does not start with a backslash.

\alph{*counter*}
> Print the value of *counter* in lowercase letters: 'a', 'b', ...

\Alph{*counter*}
> Print in uppercase letters: 'A', 'B', ...

\arabic{*counter*}
> Print in Arabic numbers: '1', '2', ...

\roman{*counter*}
> Print in lowercase roman numerals: 'i', 'ii', ...

\Roman{*counter*}
> Print in uppercase roman numerals: 'I', 'II', ...

\fnsymbol{*counter*}
> Prints the value of *counter* in a specific sequence of nine symbols (conventionally used for labeling footnotes). The value of *counter* must be between 1 and 9, inclusive.
>
> Here are the symbols:

Name	Command	Symbol
asterisk	\ast	∗
dagger	\dagger	†
ddagger	\ddagger	‡
section-sign	\S	§
paragraph-sign	\P	¶
double-vert	\parallel	‖
double-asterisk	\ast\ast	∗∗
double-dagger	\dagger\dagger	††
double-ddagger	\ddagger\ddagger	‡‡

13.2 \usecounter{*counter*}

Synopsis:

> \usecounter{*counter*}

In the `list` environment, when used in the second argument, this command sets up *counter* to number the list items. It initializes *counter* to zero, and arranges that when \item is called without its optional argument then *counter* is incremented by \refstepcounter, making its value be the current `ref` value. This command is fragile (see Section 12.9 [\protect], page 78).

Put in the preamble, this makes a new list environment enumerated with *testcounter*:

```
\newcounter{testcounter}
\newenvironment{test}{%
  \begin{list}{}{%
    \usecounter{testcounter}
  }
}{%
  \end{list}
}
```

13.3 \value{*counter*}

Synopsis:

> \value{*counter*}

This command expands to the value of *counter*. It is often used in \setcounter or \addtocounter, but \value can be used anywhere that LATEX expects a number. It must not be preceded by \protect (see Section 12.9 [\protect], page 78).

The \value command is not used for typesetting the value of the counter. See Section 13.1 [\alph \Alph \arabic \roman \Roman \fnsymbol], page 80.

This example outputs 'Test counter is 6. Other counter is 5.'.

```
\newcounter{test} \setcounter{test}{5}
\newcounter{other} \setcounter{other}{\value{test}}
\addtocounter{test}{1}

Test counter is \arabic{test}.
Other counter is \arabic{other}.
```

This example inserts `\hspace{4\parindent}`.

```
\setcounter{myctr}{3} \addtocounter{myctr}{1}
\hspace{\value{myctr}\parindent}
```

13.4 `\setcounter{`*counter*`}{`*value*`}`

Synopsis:

```
\setcounter{counter}{value}
```

The `\setcounter` command globally sets the value of *counter* to the *value* argument. Note that the counter name does not start with a backslash.

In this example the section value appears as 'V'.

```
\setcounter{section}{5}
Here it is in Roman: \Roman{section}.
```

13.5 `\addtocounter{`*counter*`}{`*value*`}`

The `\addtocounter` command globally increments *counter* by the amount specified by the *value* argument, which may be negative.

In this example the section value appears as 'VII'.

```
\setcounter{section}{5}
\addtocounter{section}{2}
Here it is in Roman: \Roman{section}.
```

13.6 `\refstepcounter{`*counter*`}`

The `\refstepcounter` command works in the same way as `\stepcounter` (see Section 13.7 [\stepcounter], page 82): it globally increments the value of *counter* by one and resets the value of any counter numbered within it. (For the definition of "counters numbered within", see Section 12.3 [\newcounter], page 73.)

In addition, this command also defines the current `\ref` value to be the result of `\thecounter`.

While the counter value is set globally, the `\ref` value is set locally, i.e., inside the current group.

13.7 `\stepcounter{`*counter*`}`

The `\stepcounter` command globally adds one to *counter* and resets all counters numbered within it. (For the definition of "counters numbered within", see Section 12.3 [\newcounter], page 73.)

13.8 `\day` `\month` `\year`: **Predefined counters**

LaTeX defines counters for the day of the month (`\day`, 1–31), month of the year (`\month`, 1–12), and year (`\year`, Common Era). When TeX starts up, they are set to the current values on the system where TeX is running. They are not updated as the job progresses.

The related command `\today` produces a string representing the current day (see Section 21.8 [\today], page 120).

14 Lengths

A *length* is a measure of distance. Many LaTeX commands take a length as an argument.

Lengths come in two types. A *rigid length* (what Plain TeX calls a *dimen*) such as `10pt` cannot contain a `plus` or `minus` component. A *rubber length* (what Plain TeX calls a *skip*) can contain those, as with `1cm plus0.05cm minus0.01cm`. These give the ability to stretch or shrink; the length in the prior sentence could appear in the output as long as 1.05 cm or as short as 0.99 cm, depending on what TeX's typesetting algorithm finds optimum.

The `plus` or `minus` component of a rubber length can contain a *fill* component, as in `1in plus2fill`. This gives the length infinite stretchability or shrinkability, so that the length in the prior sentence can be set by TeX to any distance greater than or equal to 1 inch. TeX actually provides three infinite glue components `fil`, `fill`, and `filll`, such that the later ones overcome the earlier ones, but only the middle value is ordinarily used. See Section 19.2 [\hfill], page 107, See Section 19.11 [\vfill], page 110.

Multiplying an entire rubber length by a number turns it into a rigid length, so that after `\setlength{\ylength}{1in plus 0.2in}` and `\setlength{\zlength}{3\ylength}` then the value of `\zlength` is `3in`.

14.1 Units of length

TeX and LaTeX know about these units both inside and outside of math mode.

pt   Point 1/72.27 inch. The conversion to metric units, to two decimal places, is 1 point = 2.85 mm = 28.45 cm.

pc   Pica, 12 pt

in   Inch, 72.27 pt

bp   Big point, 1/72 inch. This length is the definition of a point in PostScript and many desktop publishing systems.

cm   Centimeter

mm   Millimeter

dd   Didot point, 1.07 pt

cc   Cicero, 12 dd

sp   Scaled point, 1/65536 pt

Two other lengths that are often used are values set by the designer of the font. The x-height of the current font *ex*, traditionally the height of the lower case letter x, is often used for vertical lengths. Similarly *em*, traditionally the width of the capital letter M, is often used for horizontal lengths (there is also `\enspace`, which is `0.5em`). Use of these can help make a definition work better across font changes. For example, a definition of the vertical space between list items given as `\setlength{\itemsep}{1ex plus 0.05ex minus 0.01ex}` is more likely to still be reasonable if the font is changed than a definition given in points.

In math mode, many definitions are expressed in terms of the math unit *mu* given by 1 em = 18 mu, where the em is taken from the current math symbols family. See Section 16.5 [Spacing in math mode], page 100.

14.2 \setlength

Synopsis:

> \setlength{\len}{amount}

The \setlength sets the value of *length command* \len to the *value* argument which can be expressed in any units that LaTeX understands, i.e., inches (in), millimeters (mm), points (pt), big points (bp), etc.

14.3 \addtolength

Synopsis:

> \addtolength{\len}{amount}

The \addtolength command increments a length command \len by the amount specified in the *amount* argument, which may be negative.

14.4 \settodepth

Synopsis:

> \settodepth{\len}{text}

The \settodepth command sets the value of a length command \len equal to the depth of the *text* argument.

14.5 \settoheight

Synopsis:

> \settoheight{\len}{text}

The \settoheight command sets the value of a length command \len equal to the height of the text argument.

14.6 \settowidth{\len}{text}

Synopsis:

> \settowidth{\len}{text}

The \settowidth command sets the value of the command \len to the width of the *text* argument.

14.7 Predefined lengths

\width

  \height

  \depth

  \totalheight

These length parameters can be used in the arguments of the box-making commands (see Chapter 20 [Boxes], page 111). They specify the natural width, etc., of the text in the box. \totalheight equals \height + \depth. To make a box with the text stretched to double the natural size, e.g., say

> \makebox[2\width]{Get a stretcher}

15 Making paragraphs

A paragraph is ended by one or more completely blank lines—lines not containing even a %. A blank line should not appear where a new paragraph cannot be started, such as in math mode or in the argument of a sectioning command.

15.1 \indent

\indent produces a horizontal space whose width equals to the \parindent length, the normal paragraph indentation. It is used to add paragraph indentation where it would otherwise be suppressed.

The default value for \parindent is 1em in two-column mode, otherwise 15pt for 10pt documents, 17pt for 11pt, and 1.5em for 12pt.

15.2 \noindent

When used at the beginning of the paragraph, this command suppresses any paragraph indentation, as in this example.

```
... end of the prior paragraph.

\noindent This paragraph is not indented.
```

It has no effect when used in the middle of a paragraph.

To eliminate paragraph indentation in an entire document, put \setlength{\parindent}{0pt} in the preamble.

15.3 \parskip

\parskip is a rubber length defining extra vertical space added before each paragraph. The default is 0pt plus1pt.

15.4 Marginal notes

Synopsis:

```
\marginpar[left]{right}
```

The \marginpar command creates a note in the margin. The first line of the note will have the same baseline as the line in the text where the \marginpar occurs.

When you only specify the mandatory argument *right*, the text will be placed

- in the right margin for one-sided layout (option oneside, see Section 3.1 [Document class options], page 8);

- in the outside margin for two-sided layout (option twoside, see Section 3.1 [Document class options], page 8);

- in the nearest margin for two-column layout (option twocolumn, see Section 3.1 [Document class options], page 8).

The command \reversemarginpar places subsequent marginal notes in the opposite (inside) margin. \normalmarginpar places them in the default position.

When you specify both arguments, *left* is used for the left margin, and *right* is used for the right margin.

The first word will normally not be hyphenated; you can enable hyphenation there by beginning the node with `\hspace{0pt}`.

These parameters affect the formatting of the note:

`\marginparpush`

> Minimum vertical space between notes; default '7pt' for '12pt' documents, '5pt' else.

`\marginparsep`

> Horizontal space between the main text and the note; default '11pt' for '10pt' documents, '10pt' else.

`\marginparwidth`

> Width of the note itself; default for a one-sided '10pt' document is '90pt', '83pt' for '11pt', and '68pt' for '12pt'; '17pt' more in each case for a two-sided document. In two column mode, the default is '48pt'.

The standard LaTeX routine for marginal notes does not prevent notes from falling off the bottom of the page.

16 Math formulas

There are three environments that put LaTeX in math mode:

math   For formulas that appear right in the text.

displaymath
            For formulas that appear on their own line.

equation   The same as the displaymath environment except that it adds an equation
            number in the right margin.

The `math` environment can be used in both paragraph and LR mode, but the
`displaymath` and `equation` environments can be used only in paragraph mode. The `math`
and `displaymath` environments are used so often that they have the following short forms:

    \(...\)   instead of   \begin{math}...\end{math}
    \[...\]   instead of   \begin{displaymath}...\end{displaymath}

In fact, the `math` environment is so common that it has an even shorter form:

    $ ... $ instead of   \(...\)

The `\boldmath` command changes math letters and symbols to be in a bold font. It is
used *outside* of math mode. Conversely, the `\unboldmath` command changes math glyphs
to be in a normal font; it too is used *outside* of math mode.

The `\displaystyle` declaration forces the size and style of the formula to be that of
`displaymath`, e.g., with limits above and below summations. For example:

    $\displaystyle \sum_{n=0}^\infty x_n $

16.1 Subscripts & superscripts

In math mode, use the caret character ^ to make the *exp* appear as a superscript: ^{*exp*}.
Similarly, in math mode, underscore _{*exp*} makes a subscript out of *exp*.

In this example the 0 and 1 appear as subscripts while the 2 is a superscript.

    \((x_0+x_1)^2 \)

To have more than one character in *exp* use curly braces as in e^{-2x}.

LaTeX handles superscripts on superscripts, and all of that stuff, in the natural way, so
expressions such as e^{x^2} and x_{a_0} will look right. It also does the right thing when
something has both a subscript and a superscript. In this example the 0 appears at the
bottom of the integral sign while the 10 appears at the top.

    \int_0^{10} x^2 \,dx

You can put a superscript or subscript before a symbol with a construct such as {}_t
K^2 in math mode (the initial {} prevents the prefixed subscript from being attached to
any prior symbols in the expression).

Outside of math mode, a construct like A test$_\textnormal{subscript}$ will produce a subscript typeset in text mode, not math mode. Note that there are packages
specialized for writing Chemical formulas such as `mhchem`.

16.2 Math symbols

LaTeX provides almost any mathematical symbol you're likely to need. For example, if you include `$\pi$` in your source, you will get the pi symbol π.

Below is a list of commonly-available symbols. It is by no means an exhaustive list. Each symbol here is described with a short phrase, and its symbol class (which determines the spacing around it) is given in parenthesis. Unless said otherwise, the commands for these symbols can be used only in math mode.

To redefine a command so that it can be used whatever the current mode, see Section 17.1 [\ensuremath], page 103.

`\|`   Parallel (relation). Synonym: `\parallel`.

`\aleph` $\aleph$ Aleph, transfinite cardinal (ordinary).

`\alpha` α Lower case Greek letter alpha (ordinary).

`\amalg` $\amalg$ Disjoint union (binary)

`\angle` $\angle$ Geometric angle (ordinary). Similar: less-than sign < and angle bracket `\langle`.

`\approx` $\approx$ Almost equal to (relation).

`\ast`   * Asterisk operator, convolution, six-pointed (binary). Synonym: *, which is often a superscript or subscript, as in the Kleene star. Similar: `\star`, which is five-pointed, and is sometimes used as a general binary operation, and sometimes reserved for cross-correlation.

`\asymp` $\asymp$ Asymptotically equivalent (relation).

`\backslash`
            \ Backslash (ordinary). Similar: set minus `\setminus`, and `\textbackslash` for backslash outside of math mode.

`\beta` β Lower case Greek letter beta (ordinary).

`\bigcap` $\bigcap$ Variable-sized, or n-ary, intersection (operator). Similar: binary intersection `\cap`.

`\bigcirc` $\bigcirc$ Circle, larger (binary). Similar: function composition `\circ`.

`\bigcup` $\bigcup$ Variable-sized, or n-ary, union (operator). Similar: binary union `\cup`.

`\bigodot` $\bigodot$ Variable-sized, or n-ary, circled dot operator (operator).

`\bigoplus`
            $\bigoplus$ Variable-sized, or n-ary, circled plus operator (operator).

`\bigotimes`
            $\bigotimes$ Variable-sized, or n-ary, circled times operator (operator).

`\bigtriangledown`
            $\bigtriangledown$ Variable-sized, or n-ary, open triangle pointing down (operator).

`\bigtriangleup`
            $\bigtriangleup$ Variable-sized, or n-ary, open triangle pointing up (operator).

\bigsqcup

⨆ Variable-sized, or n-ary, square union (operator).

\biguplus

⨄ Variable-sized, or n-ary, union operator with a plus (operator). (Note that the name has only one p.)

\bigvee   ⋁ Variable-sized, or n-ary, logical-and (operator).

\bigwedge

⋀ Variable-sized, or n-ary, logical-or (operator).

\bot   \bot Up tack, bottom, least element of a partially ordered set, or a contradiction (ordinary). See also \top.

\bowtie   ⋈ Natural join of two relations (relation).

\Box   \Box Modal operator for necessity; square open box (ordinary). Not available in plain TeX. In LaTeX you need to load the amssymb package.

\bullet   • Bullet (binary). Similar: multiplication dot \cdot.

\cap   ∩ Intersection of two sets (binary). Similar: variable-sized operator \bigcap.

\cdot   · Multiplication (binary). Similar: Bullet dot \bullet.

\chi χ Lower case Greek chi (ordinary).

\circ   ∘ Function composition, ring operator (binary). Similar: variable-sized operator \bigcirc.

\clubsuit

♣ Club card suit (ordinary).

\complement

\complement Set complement, used as a superscript as in $S^\complement$ (ordinary). Not available in plain TeX. In LaTeX you need to load the amssymb package. Also used: S^{c} or $\bar{S}$.

\cong   ≅ Congruent (relation).

\coprod   ∐ Coproduct (operator).

\cup   ∪ Union of two sets (binary). Similar: variable-sized operator \bigcup.

\dagger   † Dagger relation (binary).

\dashv   ⊣ Dash with vertical, reversed turnstile (relation). Similar: turnstile \vdash.

\ddagger   ‡ Double dagger relation (binary).

\Delta Δ Greek upper case delta, used for increment (ordinary).

\delta δ Greek lower case delta (ordinary).

\Diamond   \Diamond Large diamond operator (ordinary). Not available in plain TeX. In LaTeX you need to load the amssymb package.

\diamond   ⋄ Diamond operator, or diamond bullet (binary). Similar: large diamond \Diamond, circle bullet \bullet.

\diamondsuit

> ◇ Diamond card suit (ordinary).

\div   ÷ Division sign (binary).

\doteq   ≐ Approaches the limit (relation). Similar: geometrically equal to \Doteq.

\downarrow

> ↓ Down arrow, converges (relation). Similar: double line down arrow \Downarrow.

\Downarrow

> ⇓ Double line down arrow (relation). Similar: single line down arrow \downarrow.

\ell   ℓ Lower-case cursive letter l (ordinary).

\emptyset

> ∅ Empty set symbol (ordinary). The variant form is \varnothing.

\epsilon   ϵ Lower case lunate epsilon (ordinary). Similar to Greek text letter. More widely used in mathematics is the script small letter epsilon \varepsilon ε. Related: the set membership relation \in ∈.

\equiv   ≡ Equivalence (relation).

\eta   η Lower case Greek letter (ordinary).

\exists   ∃ Existential quantifier (ordinary).

\flat   ♭ Musical flat (ordinary).

\forall   ∀ Universal quantifier (ordinary).

\frown   ⌢ Downward curving arc (ordinary).

\Gamma   Γ Upper case Greek letter (ordinary).

\gamma   γ Lower case Greek letter (ordinary).

\ge   ≥ Greater than or equal to (relation). This is a synonym for \geq.

\geq   ≥ Greater than or equal to (relation). This is a synonym for \ge.

\gets   ← Is assigned the value (relation). Synonym: \leftarrow.

\gg   ≫ Much greater than (relation). Similar: much less than \ll.

\hbar   ℏ Planck constant over two pi (ordinary).

\heartsuit

> ♡ Heart card suit (ordinary).

\hookleftarrow

> ↩ Hooked left arrow (relation).

\hookrightarrow

> ↪ Hooked right arrow (relation).

\iff   ⟺ If and only if (relation). It is \Longleftrightarrow with a \thickmuskip on either side.

\Im   ℑ Imaginary part (ordinary). See: real part \Re.

\in   ∈ Set element (relation). See also: lower case lunate epsilon \epsilonϵ and
              small letter script epsilon \varepsilon.

\infty   ∞ Infinity (ordinary).

\int   ∫ Integral (operator).

\iota   ι Lower case Greek letter (ordinary).

\Join   \Join Condensed bowtie symbol (relation). Not available in Plain TeX.

\kappa   κ Lower case Greek letter (ordinary).

\Lambda   Λ Upper case Greek letter (ordinary).

\lambda   λ Lower case Greek letter (ordinary).

\land   ∧ Logical and (binary). This is a synonym for \wedge. See also logical or \lor.

\langle   ⟨ Left angle, or sequence, bracket (opening). Similar: less-than <.
              Matches \rangle.

\lbrace   { Left curly brace (opening). Synonym: \{. Matches \rbrace.

\lbrack   [Left square bracket (opening). Synonym: [. Matches \rbrack.

\lceil   ⌈ Left ceiling bracket, like a square bracket but with the bottom shaved off
              (opening). Matches \rceil.

\le   ≤ Less than or equal to (relation). This is a synonym for \leq.

\leadsto   \leadsto Squiggly right arrow (relation). Not available in plain TeX. In LaTeX
              you need to load the amssymb package. To get this symbol outside of math
              mode you can put \newcommand*{\Leadsto}{\ensuremath{\leadsto}} in the
              preamble and then use \Leadsto instead.

\Leftarrow
              ⇐ Is implied by, double-line left arrow (relation). Similar: single-line left ar-
              row \leftarrow.

\leftarrow
              ← Single-line left arrow (relation). Synonym: \gets. Similar: double-line left
              arrow \Leftarrow.

\leftharpoondown
              ↽ Single-line left harpoon, barb under bar (relation).

\leftharpoonup
              ↼ Single-line left harpoon, barb over bar (relation).

\Leftrightarrow
              ⇔ Bi-implication; double-line double-headed arrow (relation). Similar: single-
              line double headed arrow \leftrightarrow.

\leftrightarrow
              ↔ Single-line double-headed arrow (relation). Similar: double-line double
              headed arrow \Leftrightarrow.

\leq   ≤ Less than or equal to (relation). This is a synonym for \le.

\lfloor   ⌊ Left floor bracket (opening). Matches: \floor.

\lhd   \lhd Arrowhead, that is, triangle, pointing left (binary). Not available in plain TeX. In LaTeX you need to load the **amssymb** package. For the normal subgroup symbol you should load **amssymb** and use \vartriangleleft (which is a relation and so gives better spacing).

\ll   ≪ Much less than (relation). Similar: much greater than \gg.

\lnot   ¬ Logical negation (ordinary). Synonym: \neg.

\longleftarrow
            ⟵ Long single-line left arrow (relation). Similar: long double-line left arrow \Longleftarrow.

\longleftrightarrow
            ⟷ Long single-line double-headed arrow (relation). Similar: long double-line double-headed arrow \Longleftrightarrow.

\longmapsto
            ⟼ Long single-line left arrow starting with vertical bar (relation). Similar: shorter version \mapsto.

\longrightarrow
            ⟶ Long single-line right arrow (relation). Similar: long double-line right arrow \Longrightarrow.

\lor   ∨ Logical or (binary). Synonym: wedge \wedge.

\mapsto   ↦ Single-line left arrow starting with vertical bar (relation). Similar: longer version \longmapsto.

\mho   \mho Conductance, half-circle rotated capital omega (ordinary). Not available in plain TeX. In LaTeX you need to load the **amssymb** package.

\mid | Single-line vertical bar (relation). A typical use of \mid is for a set \{\, x \mid x\geq 5 \,\}.

            Similar: \vert and | produce the same single-line vertical bar symbol but without any spacing (they fall in class ordinary) and you should not use them as relations but instead only as ordinals, i.e., footnote symbols. For absolute value, see the entry for \vert and for norm see the entry for \Vert.

\models   ⊨ Entails, or satisfies; double turnstile, short double dash (relation). Similar: long double dash \vDash.

\mp   ∓ Minus or plus (relation).

\mu   μ Lower case Greek letter (ordinary).

\nabla   ∇ Hamilton's del, or differential, operator (ordinary).

\natural   ♮ Musical natural notation (ordinary).

\ne   ≠ Not equal (relation). Synonym: \neq.

\nearrow   ↗ North-east arrow (relation).

\neg   ¬ Logical negation (ordinary). Synonym: \lnot. Sometimes instead used for negation: \sim.

\neq   ≠ Not equal (relation). Synonym: \ne.

\ni   ∋ Reflected membership epsilon; has the member (relation). Synonym: \owns. Similar: is a member of \in.

\not   ⁄Long solidus, or slash, used to overstrike a following operator (relation).

            Many negated operators that don't require \not are available, particularly with the amssymb package. For example, \notin is probably typographically preferable to \not\in.

\notin   ∉ Not an element of (relation). Similar: not subset of \nsubseteq.

\nu   ν Lower case Greek letter (ordinary).

\nwarrow   ↖ North-west arrow (relation).

\odot   ⊙ Dot inside a circle (binary). Similar: variable-sized operator \bigodot.

\oint   ∮ Contour integral, integral with circle in the middle (operator).

\Omega   Ω Upper case Greek letter (ordinary).

\omega   ω Lower case Greek letter (ordinary).

\ominus   ⊖ Minus sign, or dash, inside a circle (binary).

\oplus   ⊕ Plus sign inside a circle (binary). Similar: variable-sized operator \bigoplus.

\oslash   ⊘ Solidus, or slash, inside a circle (binary).

\otimes   ⊗ Times sign, or cross, inside a circle (binary). Similar: variable-sized operator \bigotimes.

\owns   ∋ Reflected membership epsilon; has the member (relation). Synonym: \ni. Similar: is a member of \in.

\parallel
            ∥ Parallel (relation). Synonym: \|.

\partial   ∂ Partial differential (ordinary).

\perp   ⊥ Perpendicular (relation). Similar: \bot uses the same glyph but the spacing is different because it is in the class ordinary.

\phi   φ Lower case Greek letter (ordinary). The variant form is \varphi φ.

\Pi   Π Upper case Greek letter (ordinary).

\pi   π Lower case Greek letter (ordinary). The variant form is \varpi ϖ.

\pm   ± Plus or minus (binary).

\prec   ≺ Precedes (relation). Similar: less than <.

\preceq   ≼ Precedes or equals (relation). Similar: less than or equals \leq.

\prime	*′* Prime, or minute in a time expression (ordinary). Typically used as a superscript: $f^\prime$; $f^\prime$ and f' produce the same result. An advantage of the second is that f''' produces the desired symbol, that is, the same result as $f^{\prime\prime\prime}$, but uses rather less typing. You can only use \prime in math mode. Using the right single quote ' in text mode produces a different character (apostrophe).
\prod	∏ Product (operator).
\propto	∝ Is proportional to (relation)
\Psi	Ψ Upper case Greek letter (ordinary).
\psi	*ψ* Lower case Greek letter (ordinary).
\rangle	⟩ Right angle, or sequence, bracket (closing). Similar: greater than >. Matches:\langle.
\rbrace	} Right curly brace (closing). Synonym: \}. Matches \lbrace.
\rbrack	] Right square bracket (closing). Synonym:]. Matches \lbrack.
\rceil	⌉ Right ceiling bracket (closing). Matches \lceil.
\Re	ℜ Real part, real numbers, cursive capital R (ordinary). Related: double-line, or blackboard bold, R \mathbb{R}; to access this, load the **amsfonts** package.

\restriction

    \restriction Restriction of a function (relation). Synonym: \upharpoonright. Not available in plain TeX. In LaTeX you need to load the **amssymb** package.

\revemptyset

    \revemptyset Reversed empty set symbol (ordinary). Related: \varnothing. Not available in plain TeX. In LaTeX you need to load the **stix** package.

\rfloor	⌋ Right floor bracket, a right square bracket with the top cut off (closing). Matches \lfloor.
\rhd	\rhd Arrowhead, that is, triangle, pointing right (binary). Not available in plain TeX. In LaTeX you need to load the **amssymb** package. For the normal subgroup symbol you should instead load **amssymb** and use \vartriangleright (which is a relation and so gives better spacing).
\rho	*ρ* Lower case Greek letter (ordinary). The variant form is \varrho *ϱ*.

\Rightarrow

    ⇒ Implies, right-pointing double line arrow (relation). Similar: right single-line arrow \rightarrow.

\rightarrow

    → Right-pointing single line arrow (relation). Synonym: \to. Similar: right double line arrow \Rightarrow.

\rightharpoondown

    ⇁ Right-pointing harpoon with barb below the line (relation).

\rightharpoonup

    ⇀ Right-pointing harpoon with barb above the line (relation).

\rightleftharpoons

⇌ Right harpoon up above left harpoon down (relation).

\searrow   ↘ Arrow pointing southeast (relation).

\setminus

\ Set difference, reverse solidus or slash, like \ (binary). Similar: backslash **\backslash** and also **\textbackslash** outside of math mode.

\sharp   ♯ Musical sharp (ordinary).

\Sigma   Σ Upper case Greek letter (ordinary).

\sigma   σ Lower case Greek letter (ordinary). The variant form is **\varsigma** ς.

\sim   ∼ Similar, in a relation (relation).

\simeq   ≃ Similar or equal to, in a relation (relation).

\smallint

∫ Integral sign that does not change to a larger size in a display (operator).

\smile   ⌣ Upward curving arc, smile (ordinary).

\spadesuit

♠ Spade card suit (ordinary).

\sqcap   ⊓ Square intersection symbol (binary). Similar: intersection **cap**.

\sqcup   ⊔ Square union symbol (binary). Similar: union **cup**. Related: variable-sized operator **\bigsqcup**.

\sqsubset

\sqsubset Square subset symbol (relation). Similar: subset **\subset**. Not available in plain TeX. In LaTeX you need to load the **amssymb** package.

\sqsubseteq

⊑ Square subset or equal symbol (binary). Similar: subset or equal to **\subseteq**.

\sqsupset

\sqsupset Square superset symbol (relation). Similar: superset **\supset**. Not available in plain TeX. In LaTeX you need to load the **amssymb** package.

\sqsupseteq

⊒ Square superset or equal symbol (binary). Similar: superset or equal **\supseteq**.

\star   ⋆ Five-pointed star, sometimes used as a general binary operation but sometimes reserved for cross-correlation (binary). Similar: the synonyms asterisk * and **\ast**, which are six-pointed, and more often appear as a superscript or subscript, as with the Kleene star.

\subset   ⊂ Subset (occasionally, is implied by) (relation).

\subseteq

⊆ Subset or equal to (relation).

\succ   ≻ Comes after, succeeds (relation). Similar: is less than >.

\succeq   ⪰ Succeeds or is equal to (relation). Similar: less than or equal to \leq.

\sum   ∑ Summation (operator). Similar: Greek capital sigma \Sigma.

\supset   ⊃ Superset (relation).

\supseteq
           ⊇ Superset or equal to (relation).

\surd   √ Radical symbol (ordinary). The LaTeX command \sqrt{...} typesets the
           square root of the argument, with a bar that extends to cover the argument.

\swarrow   ↙ Southwest-pointing arrow (relation).

\tau   τ Lower case Greek letter (ordinary).

\theta   θ Lower case Greek letter (ordinary). The variant form is \vartheta ϑ.

\times   × Primary school multiplication sign (binary). See also \cdot.

\to   → Right-pointing single line arrow (relation). Synonym: \rightarrow.

\top   \top Top, greatest element of a partially ordered set (ordinary). See also \bot.

\triangle
           △ Triangle (ordinary).

\triangleleft
           ◁ Not-filled triangle pointing left (binary). Similar: \lhd. For the normal
           subgroup symbol you should load amssymb and use \vartriangleleft (which
           is a relation and so gives better spacing).

\triangleright
           ▷ Not-filled triangle pointing right (binary). For the normal subgroup sym-
           bol you should instead load amssymb and use \vartriangleright (which is a
           relation and so gives better spacing).

\unlhd   \unlhd Left-pointing not-filled underlined arrowhead, that is, triangle, with
           a line under (binary). Not available in plain TeX. In LaTeX you need to
           load the amssymb package. For the normal subgroup symbol load amssymb
           and use \vartrianglelefteq (which is a relation and so gives better spacing).

\unrhd   \unrhd Right-pointing not-filled underlined arrowhead, that is, triangle, with a
           line under (binary). Not available in plain TeX. In LaTeX you need to load
           the amssymb package. For the normal subgroup symbol load amssymb and
           use \vartrianglerighteq (which is a relation and so gives better spacing).

\Uparrow   ⇑ Double-line upward-pointing arrow (relation). Similar: single-line
           up-pointing arrow \uparrow.

\uparrow   ↑ Single-line upward-pointing arrow, diverges (relation). Similar: double-line
           up-pointing arrow \Uparrow.

\Updownarrow
           ⇕ Double-line upward-and-downward-pointing arrow (relation). Similar: single-
           line upward-and-downward-pointing arrow \updownarrow.

\updownarrow

> ↕ Single-line upward-and-downward-pointing arrow (relation). Similar: double-line upward-and-downward-pointing arrow \Updownarrow.

\upharpoonright

> \upharpoonright Up harpoon, with barb on right side (relation). Synonym: \restriction. Not available in plain TeX. In LaTeX you need to load the amssymb package.

\uplus   ⊎ Multiset union, a union symbol with a plus symbol in the middle (binary). Similar: union \cup. Related: variable-sized operator \biguplus.

\Upsilon   ϒ Upper case Greek letter (ordinary).

\upsilon   υ Lower case Greek letter (ordinary).

\varepsilon

> ε Small letter script epsilon (ordinary). This is more widely used in mathematics than the non-variant lunate epsilon form \epsilon ϵ. Related: set membership \in.

\vanothing

> \varnothing Empty set symbol. Similar: \emptyset. Related: \revemptyset. Not available in plain TeX. In LaTeX you need to load the amssymb package.

\varphi   φ Variant on the lower case Greek letter (ordinary). The non-variant form is \phi ϕ.

\varpi   ϖ Variant on the lower case Greek letter (ordinary). The non-variant form is \pi π.

\varrho   ϱ Variant on the lower case Greek letter (ordinary). The non-variant form is \rho ρ.

\varsigma

> ς Variant on the lower case Greek letter (ordinary). The non-variant form is \sigma σ.

\vartheta

> ϑ Variant on the lower case Greek letter (ordinary). The non-variant form is \theta θ.

\vdash   ⊢ Provable; turnstile, vertical and a dash (relation). Similar: turnstile rotated a half-circle \dashv.

\vee   ∨ Logical or; a downwards v shape (binary). Related: logical and \wedge. Similar: variable-sized operator \bigvee.

\Vert   ‖ Vertical double bar (ordinary). Similar: vertical single bar \vert.

> For a norm symbol, you can use the mathtools package and add \DeclarePairedDelimiter\norm{\lVert}{\rVert} to your preamble. This gives you three command variants for double-line vertical bars that are correctly horizontally spaced: if in the document body you write the starred version $\norm*{M^\perp}$ then the height of the vertical bars will match

the height of the argument, whereas with `\norm{M^\perp}` the bars do not grow with the height of the argument but instead are the default height, and `\norm[size command]{M^\perp}` also gives bars that do not grow but are set to the size given in the *size command*, e.g., `\Bigg`.

`\vert`	| Single line vertical bar (ordinary). Similar: double-line vertical bar `\Vert`. For such that, as in the definition of a set, use `\mid` because it is a relation.

For absolute value you can use the `mathtools` package and add `\DeclarePairedDelimiter\abs{\lvert}{\rvert}` to your preamble. This gives you three command variants for single-line vertical bars that are correctly horizontally spaced: if in the document body you write the starred version `$\abs*{\frac{22}{7}}$` then the height of the vertical bars will match the height of the argument, whereas with `\abs{\frac{22}{7}}` the bars do not grow with the height of the argument but instead are the default height, and `\abs[size command]{\frac{22}{7}}` also gives bars that do not grow but are set to the size given in the *size command*, e.g., `\Bigg`.

`\wedge`	$\wedge$ Logical and (binary). Synonym: `\land`. See also logical or `\vee`. Similar: variable-sized operator `\bigwedge`.
`\wp`	$\wp$ Weierstrass p (ordinary).
`\wr`	$\wr$ Wreath product (binary).
`\Xi`	Ξ Upper case Greek letter (ordinary).
`\xi`	ξ Lower case Greek letter (ordinary).
`\zeta`	ζ Lower case Greek letter (ordinary).

16.3 Math functions

These commands produce roman function names in math mode with proper spacing.

`\arccos`	arccos
`\arcsin`	arcsin
`\arctan`	arctan
`\arg`	arg
`\bmod`	Binary modulo operator ($x \bmod y$)
`\cos`	cos
`\cosh`	cosh
`\cot`	cot
`\coth`	coth
`\csc`	csc
`\deg`	deg
`\det`	det

\dim	dim
\exp	exp
\gcd	gcd
\hom	hom
\inf	inf
\ker	ker
\lg	lg
\lim	lim
\liminf	lim inf
\limsup	lim sup
\ln	ln
\log	log
\max	max
\min	min
\pmod	parenthesized modulus, as in $(\pmod 2)^n - 1$
\Pr	Pr
\sec	sec
\sin	sin
\sinh	sinh
\sup	sup
\tan	tan
\tanh	tanh

16.4 Math accents

LaTeX provides a variety of commands for producing accented letters in math. These are different from accents in normal text (see Section 21.5 [Accents], page 118).

\acute	Math acute accent: $\acute{x}$.
\bar	Math bar-over accent: $\bar{x}$.
\breve	Math breve accent: $\breve{x}$.
\check	Math háček (check) accent: $\check{x}$.
\ddot	Math dieresis accent: $\ddot{x}$.
\dot	Math dot accent: $\dot{x}$.
\grave	Math grave accent: $\grave{x}$.

\hat	Math hat (circumflex) accent: $\hat{x}$.
\imath	Math dotless i.
\jmath	Math dotless j.
\mathring	
	Math ring accent: $\mathring{x}$.
\tilde	Math tilde accent: $\tilde{x}$.
\vec	Math vector symbol: $\vec{x}$.
\widehat	Math wide hat accent: $\widehat{x+y}$.
\widetilde	
	Math wide tilde accent: $\widetilde{x+y}$.

16.5 Spacing in math mode

In a `math` environment, LaTeX ignores the spaces that you use in the source, and instead puts in the spacing according to the normal rules for mathematics texts.

Many math mode spacing definitions are expressed in terms of the math unit *mu* given by 1 em = 18 mu, where the em is taken from the current math symbols family (see Section 14.1 [Units of length], page 83). LaTeX provides the following commands for use in math mode:

\;	Normally `5.0mu plus 5.0mu`. The longer name is `\thickspace`. Math mode only.
\:	
\>	Normally `4.0mu plus 2.0mu minus 4.0mu`. The longer name is `\medspace`. Math mode only.
\,	Normally `3mu`. The longer name is `\thinspace`. This can be used in both math mode and text mode. See Section 19.6 [\thinspace], page 108.
\!	A negative thin space. Normally `-3mu`. Math mode only.
\quad	This is 18 mu, that is, 1 em. This is often used for space surrounding equations or expressions, for instance for the space between two equations inside a `displaymath` environment. It is available in both text and math mode.
\qquad	A length of 2 quads, that is, 36 mu = 2 em. It is available in both text and math mode.

In this example a thinspace separates the function from the infinitesimal.

```
\int_0^1 f(x)\,dx
```

16.6 Math miscellany

*	A *discretionary* multiplication symbol, at which a line break is allowed. Without the break multiplication is implicitly indicated by a space, while in the case of a break a $\times$ symbol is printed immediately before the break. So

```
\documentclass{article}
```

```
\begin{document}
Now \(A_3 = 0\), hence the product of all terms \(A_1\)
through \(A_4\), that is \(A_1\* A_2\* A_3 \* A_4\), is
equal to zero.
\end{document}
```

will make that sort of output:

> Now $A_3 = 0$, hence the product of all terms A_1 through A_4, that is $A_1 A_2 \times A_3 A_4$, is equal to zero.

`\cdots`   A horizontal ellipsis with the dots raised to the center of the line. As in: '$\cdots$'.

`\ddots`   A diagonal ellipsis: $\ddots$.

`\frac{num}{den}`
   Produces the fraction *num* divided by *den*.

   eg. $\frac{1}{4}$

`\left deliml ... \right delim2`
   The two delimiters need not match; '.' acts as a *null delimiter*, producing no output. The delimiters are sized according to the math in between. Example: `\left( \sum_{i=1}^{10} a_i \right]`.

`\mathdollar`
   Dollar sign in math mode: $.

`\mathellipsis`
   Ellipsis (spaced for text) in math mode: $\ldots$.

`\mathparagraph`
   Paragraph sign (pilcrow) in math mode: ¶.

`\mathsection`
   Section sign in math mode.

`\mathsterling`
   Sterling sign in math mode: £.

`\mathunderscore`
   Underscore in math mode: _.

`\overbrace{math}`
   Generates a brace over *math*. For example, `\overbrace{x+\cdots+x}^{k \;\textrm{times}}`. The result looks like: $\overbrace{x + \cdots + x}^{k \text{ times}}$

`\overline{text}`
   Generates a horizontal line over *tex*. For example, `\overline{x+y}`. The result looks like: $\overline{x + y}$.

`\sqrt[root]{arg}`
   Produces the representation of the square root of *arg*. The optional argument *root* determines what root to produce. For example, the cube root of x+y would be typed as `\sqrt[3]{x+y}`. The result looks like this: $\sqrt[3]{x + y}$.

`\stackrel{text}{relation}`

> Puts *text* above *relation*. For example, `\stackrel{f}{\longrightarrow}`. The result looks like this: $\stackrel{f}{\longrightarrow}$.

`\underbrace{math}`

> Generates *math* with a brace underneath. For example, `\underbrace{x+y+z}_{>\,0}` The result looks like this: $\underbrace{x+y+z}_{>0}$.

`\underline{text}`

> Causes *text*, which may be either math mode or not, to be underlined. The line is always below the text, taking account of descenders. The result looks like this: $\underline{xyz}$

`\vdots`   Produces a vertical ellipsis. The result looks like this: $\vdots$.

17 Modes

When LaTeX is processing your input text, it is always in one of three modes:

- Paragraph mode
- Math mode
- Left-to-right mode, called LR mode for short

Mode changes occur only when entering or leaving an environment, or when LaTeX is processing the argument of certain text-producing commands.

Paragraph mode is the most common; it's the one LaTeX is in when processing ordinary text. In this mode, LaTeX breaks the input text into lines and breaks the lines into pages.

LaTeX is in *math mode* when it's generating a mathematical formula, either displayed math or within a line.

In *LR mode*, as in paragraph mode, LaTeX considers the output that it produces to be a string of words with spaces between them. However, unlike paragraph mode, LaTeX keeps going from left to right; it never starts a new line in LR mode. Even if you put a hundred words into an `\mbox`, LaTeX would keep typesetting them from left to right inside a single box (and then most likely complain because the resulting box was too wide to fit on the line). LaTeX is in LR mode when it starts making a box with an `\mbox` command. You can get it to enter a different mode inside the box—for example, you can make it enter math mode to put a formula in the box.

There are also several text-producing commands and environments for making a box that put LaTeX into paragraph mode. The box made by one of these commands or environments will be called a `parbox`. When LaTeX is in paragraph mode while making a box, it is said to be in "inner paragraph mode" (no page breaks). Its normal paragraph mode, which it starts out in, is called "outer paragraph mode".

17.1 \ensuremath

Synopsis:

```
\ensuremath{formula}
```

The `\ensuremath` command ensures that *formula* is typeset in math mode whatever the current mode in which the command is used.

For instance:

```
\documentclass{report}
\newcommand{\ab}{\ensuremath{(\delta, \varepsilon)}}
\begin{document}
Now, the \ab\ pair is equal to \(\ab = (\frac{1}{\pi}, 0)\), ...
\end{document}
```

One can redefine commands that can be used only in math mode so that they ca be used in any mode like in the following example given for `\leadsto`:

```
\documentclass{report}
\usepackage{amssymb}
\newcommand{\originalMeaningOfLeadsTo}{}
\let\originalMeaningOfLeadsTo\leadsto
```

```
\renewcommand\leadsto{\ensuremath{\originalMeaningOfLeadsTo}}
\begin{document}
All roads \leadsto\ Rome.
\end{document}
```

18 Page styles

The \documentclass command determines the size and position of the page's head and foot. The page style determines what goes in them.

18.1 \maketitle

The \maketitle command generates a title on a separate title page—except in the article class, where the title is placed at the top of the first page. Information used to produce the title is obtained from the following declarations:

\author{*name* \and *name2*}
> The \author command declares the document author(s), where the argument is a list of authors separated by \and commands. Use \\ to separate lines within a single author's entry—for example, to give the author's institution or address.

\date{*text*}
> The \date command declares *text* to be the document's date. With no \date command, the current date (see Section 21.8 [\today], page 120) is used.

\thanks{*text*}
> The \thanks command produces a \footnote to the title, usually used for credit acknowledgements.

\title{*text*}
> The \title command declares *text* to be the title of the document. Use \\ to force a line break, as usual.

18.2 \pagenumbering

Synopsis:

> \pagenumbering{*style*}

Specifies the style of page numbers, according to *style*; also resets the page number to 1. The *style* argument is one of the following:

arabic   arabic numerals

roman   lowercase Roman numerals

Roman   uppercase Roman numerals

alph   lowercase letters

Alph   uppercase letters

18.3 \pagestyle

Synopsis:

> \pagestyle{*style*}

The \pagestyle command specifies how the headers and footers are typeset from the current page onwards. Values for *style*:

plain   Just a plain page number.

empty   Empty headers and footers, e.g., no page numbers.

headings   Put running headers on each page. The document style specifies what goes in the headers.

myheadings
             Custom headers, specified via the \markboth or the \markright commands.

Here are the descriptions of \markboth and \markright:

\markboth{*left*}{*right*}
             Sets both the left and the right heading. A "left-hand heading" (*left*) is generated by the last \markboth command before the end of the page, while a "right-hand heading" (*right*) is generated by the first \markboth or \markright that comes on the page if there is one, otherwise by the last one before the page.

\markright{*right*}
             Sets the right heading, leaving the left heading unchanged.

18.4 \thispagestyle{*style*}

The \thispagestyle command works in the same manner as the \pagestyle command (see previous section) except that it changes to *style* for the current page only.

19 Spaces

LaTeX has many ways to produce white (or filled) space.

19.1 \hspace

Synopsis:

    \hspace{length}
    \hspace*{length}

Add the horizontal space given by *length*. The *length* is a rubber length, that is, it may contain a `plus` or `minus` component, in any unit that LaTeX understands (see Chapter 14 [Lengths], page 83).

This command can add both positive and negative space; adding negative space is like backspacing.

Normally when TeX breaks a paragraph into lines it discards white space (glues and kerns) that would come at the start of a line, so you get an inter-word space or a line break between words but not both. This command's starred version `\hspace*{...}` puts a non-discardable invisible item in front of the space, so the space appears in the output.

This example make a one-line paragraph that puts 'Name:' an inch from the right margin.

    \noindent\makebox[\linewidth]{\hspace{\fill}Name:\hspace{1in}}

19.2 \hfill

Produce a rubber length which has no natural space but can stretch horizontally as far as needed (see Chapter 14 [Lengths], page 83).

The command `\hfill` is equivalent to `\hspace{\fill}`. For space that does not disappear at line breaks use `\hspace*{\fill}` instead (see Section 19.1 [\hspace], page 107).

19.3 \(SPACE) and \@

Mark a punctuation character, typically a period, as either ending a sentence or as ending an abbreviation.

By default, in justifying a line LaTeX adjusts the space after a sentence-ending period (or a question mark, exclamation point, comma, or colon) more than the space between words (see Section 19.5 [\frenchspacing], page 108). LaTeX assumes that the period ends a sentence unless it is preceded by a capital letter, in which case it takes that period for part of an abbreviation. Note that if a sentence-ending period is immediately followed by a right parenthesis or bracket, or right single or double quote, then the inter-sentence space follows that parenthesis or quote.

If you have a period ending an abbreviation whose last letter is not a capital letter, and that abbreviation is not the last word in the sentence, then follow that period with a backslash-space (\ ) or a tie (~). Examples are `Nat.\ Acad.\ Science`, and `Mr.~Bean`, and `(manure, etc.)\ for sale`.

For another use of \ , see Section 19.4 [\(SPACE) after control sequence], page 108.

In the opposite situation, if you have a capital letter followed by a period that ends the sentence, then put `\@` before that period. For example, `book by the MAA\@.` will have inter-sentence spacing after the period.

In contrast, putting `\@` after a period tells TeX that the period does not end the sentence. In the example `reserved words (if, then, etc.\@) are different`, TeX will put interword space after the closing parenthesis (note that `\@` is before the parenthesis).

19.4 \ after control sequence

The `\` command is often used after control sequences to keep them from gobbling the space that follows, as in '`\TeX\ is nice`'. And, under normal circumstances, `\tab` and `\newline` are equivalent to `\ `. For another use of `\ `, see also Section 19.3 [\(SPACE) and \@], page 107.

Some people prefer to use `{}` for the same purpose, as in `\TeX{} is nice`. This has the advantage that you can always write it the same way, namely `\TeX{}`, whether it is followed by a space or by a punctuation mark. Compare:

```
\TeX\ is a nice system. \TeX, a nice system.
```

```
\TeX{} is a nice system. \TeX{}, a nice system.
```

Some individual commands, notably those defined with the `xspace`, package do not follow the standard behavior.

19.5 \frenchspacing

This declaration (from Plain TeX) causes LaTeX to treat inter-sentence spacing in the same way as interword spacing.

In justifying the text in a line, some typographic traditions, including English, prefer to adjust the space between sentences (or after other punctuation marks) more than the space between words. Following this declaration, all spaces are instead treated equally.

Revert to the default behavior by declaring `\nonfrenchspacing`.

19.6 \thinspace: Insert 1/6 em

`\thinspace` produces an unbreakable and unstretchable space that is 1/6 of an em. This is the proper space to use between nested quotes, as in ' ".

19.7 \/: Insert italic correction

The `\/` command produces an *italic correction*. This is a small space defined by the font designer for a given character, to avoid the character colliding with whatever follows. The italic f character typically has a large italic correction value.

If the following character is a period or comma, it's not necessary to insert an italic correction, since those punctuation symbols have a very small height. However, with semicolons or colons, as well as normal letters, it can help. Compare $f: f;$ with $f: f;$.

When changing fonts with commands such as `\textit{italic text}` or `{\itshape italic text}`, LaTeX will automatically insert an italic correction if appropriate (see Section 4.1 [Font styles], page 17).

Despite the name, roman characters can also have an italic correction. Compare pdfTEX with pdfTEX.

There is no concept of italic correction in math mode; spacing is done in a different way.

19.8 \hrulefill \dotfill

Produce an infinite rubber length (see Chapter 14 [Lengths], page 83) filled with a horizontal rule (that is, a line) or with dots, instead of just white space.

When placed between blank lines this example creates a paragraph that is left and right justified, where the space in the middle is filled with evenly spaced dots.

```
\noindent Jack Aubrey\dotfill Melbury Lodge
```

To make the rule or dots go to the line's end use \null at the start or end.

To change the rule's thickness, copy the definition and adjust it, as with `\renewcommand{\hrulefill}{\leavevmode\leaders\hrule height 1pt\hfill\kern\z@}`, which changes the default thickness of 0.4 pt to 1 pt. Similarly, adjust the dot spacing as with `\renewcommand{\dotfill}{\leavevmode\cleaders\hb@xt@ 1.00em{\hss .\hss }\hfill\kern\z@}`, which changes the default length of 0.33 em to 1.00 em.

19.9 \addvspace

`\addvspace{length}`

Add a vertical space of height *length*, which is a rubber length (see Chapter 14 [Lengths], page 83). However, if vertical space has already been added to the same point in the output by a previous \addvspace command then this command will not add more space than what is needed to make the natural length of the total vertical space equal to *length*.

Use this command to adjust the vertical space above or below an environment that starts a new paragraph. For instance, a Theorem environment is defined to begin and end with \addvspace{...} so that two consecutive Theorem's are separated by one vertical space, not two.

This command is fragile (see Section 12.9 [\protect], page 78).

The error 'Something's wrong--perhaps a missing \item' means that you were not in vertical mode when you invoked this command; one way to change that is to precede this command with a \par command.

19.10 \bigskip \medskip \smallskip

These commands produce a given amount of space, specified by the document class.

\bigskip   The same as \vspace{\bigskipamount}, ordinarily about one line space, with stretch and shrink (the default for the book and article classes is 12pt plus 4pt minus 4pt).

\medskip   The same as \vspace{\medskipamount}, ordinarily about half of a line space, with stretch and shrink (the default for the book and article classes is 6pt plus 2pt minus 2pt).

`\smallskip`

> The same as `\vspace{\smallskipamount}`, ordinarily about a quarter of a line space, with stretch and shrink (the default for the `book` and `article` classes is `3pt plus 1pt minus 1pt`).

19.11 `\vfill`

End the current paragraph and insert a vertical rubber length (see Chapter 14 [Lengths], page 83) that is infinite, so it can stretch or shrink as far as needed.

It is often used in the same way as `\vspace{\fill}`, except that `\vfill` ends the current paragraph, whereas `\vspace{\fill}` adds the infinite vertical space below its line irrespective of the paragraph structure. In both cases that space will disappear at a page boundary; to circumvent this see Section 19.12 [\vspace], page 110.

In this example the page is filled, so the top and bottom lines contain the text 'Lost Dog!' and the third 'Lost Dog!' is exactly halfway between them.

```
\begin{document}
Lost Dog!
\vfill
Lost Dog!
\vfill
Lost Dog!
\end{document}
```

19.12 `\vspace{length}`

Synopsis, one of these two:

```
\vspace{length}
\vspace*{length}
```

Add the vertical space *length*. This can be negative or positive, and is a rubber length (see Chapter 14 [Lengths], page 83).

LaTeX removes the vertical space from `\vspace` at a page break, that is, at the top or bottom of a page. The starred version `\vspace*{...}` causes the space to stay.

If `\vspace` is used in the middle of a paragraph (i.e., in horizontal mode), the space is inserted *after* the line with the `\vspace` command. A new paragraph is not started.

In this example the two questions will be evenly spaced vertically on the page, with at least one inch of space below each.

```
\begin{document}
1) Who put the bomp in the bomp bah bomp bah bomp?
\vspace{1in plus 1fill}

2) Who put the ram in the rama lama ding dong?
\vspace{1in plus 1fill}
\end{document}
```

20 Boxes

All the predefined length parameters (see Section 14.7 [Predefined lengths], page 84) can be used in the arguments of the box-making commands.

20.1 \mbox{*text*}

The \mbox command creates a box just wide enough to hold the text created by its argument. The *text* is not broken into lines, so it can be used to prevent hyphenation.

20.2 \fbox and \framebox

Synopses:

```
\fbox{text}
\framebox[width][position]{text}
```

The \fbox and \framebox commands are like \mbox, except that they put a frame around the outside of the box being created.

In addition, the \framebox command allows for explicit specification of the box width with the optional *width* argument (a dimension), and positioning with the optional *position* argument.

Both commands produce a rule of thickness \fboxrule (default '.4pt'), and leave a space of \fboxsep (default '3pt') between the rule and the contents of the box.

See Section 8.19.3 [\framebox (picture)], page 51, for the \framebox command in the picture environment.

20.3 lrbox

Synopsis:

```
\begin{lrbox}{\cmd}
  text
\end{lrbox}
```

This is the environment form of Section 20.8 [\sbox], page 113.

The *text* inside the environment is saved in the box \cmd, which must have been declared with \newsavebox.

20.4 \makebox

Synopsis:

```
\makebox[width][position]{text}
```

The \makebox command creates a box just wide enough to contain the *text* specified. The width of the box can be overridden by the optional *width* argument. The position of the text within the box is determined by the optional *position* argument, which may take the following values:

c   Centered (default).

l   Flush left.

r   Flush right.

s   Stretch (justify) across entire *width*; *text* must contain stretchable space for
            this to work.

   `\makebox` is also used within the `picture` environment see Section 8.19.2 [\makebox
(picture)], page 51.

20.5 \parbox

Synopsis:

   `\parbox[position] [height] [inner-pos]{width}{text}`

   The `\parbox` command produces a box whose contents are created in *paragraph mode*. It
should be used to make a box small pieces of text, with nothing fancy inside. In particular,
you shouldn't use any paragraph-making environments inside a `\parbox` argument. For
larger pieces of text, including ones containing a paragraph-making environment, you should
use a `minipage` environment (see Section 8.18 [minipage], page 49).

   `\parbox` has two mandatory arguments:

width   the width of the parbox;

text   the text that goes inside the parbox.

   By default LATEX will position vertically a parbox so its center lines up with the center
of the surrounding text line. When the optional *position* argument is present and equal
either to 't' or 'b', this allows you respectively to align either the top or bottom line in the
parbox with the baseline of the surrounding text. You may also specify 'm' for *position* to
get the default behaviour.

   The optional *height* argument overrides the natural height of the box.

   The *inner-pos* argument controls the placement of the text inside the box, as follows; if
it is not specified, *position* is used.

t   text is placed at the top of the box.

c   text is centered in the box.

b   text is placed at the bottom of the box.

s   stretch vertically; the text must contain vertically stretchable space for this to
            work.

20.6 \raisebox

Synopsis:

   `\raisebox{distance}[height] [depth]{text}`

   The `\raisebox` command raises or lowers *text*. The first mandatory argument specifies
how high *text* is to be raised (or lowered if it is a negative amount). *text* itself is processed
in LR mode.

   The optional arguments *height* and *depth* are dimensions. If they are specified, LATEX
treats *text* as extending a certain distance above the baseline (*height*) or below (*depth*),
ignoring its natural height and depth.

20.7 \savebox

Synopsis:

> \savebox{\boxcmd}[width] [pos]{text}

This command typeset *text* in a box just as with \makebox (see Section 20.4 [\makebox], page 111), except that instead of printing the resulting box, it saves it in the box labeled \boxcmd, which must have been declared with \newsavebox (see Section 12.5 [\newsavebox], page 74).

20.8 \sbox{\boxcmd}{text}

Synopsis:

> \sbox{\boxcmd}{text}

\sbox types *text* in a box just as with \mbox (see Section 20.1 [\mbox], page 111) except that instead of the resulting box being included in the normal output, it is saved in the box labeled \boxcmd. \boxcmd must have been previously declared with \newsavebox (see Section 12.5 [\newsavebox], page 74).

20.9 \usebox{\boxcmd}

Synopsis:

> \usebox{\boxcmd}

\usebox produces the box most recently saved in the bin \boxcmd by a \savebox command (see Section 20.7 [\savebox], page 113).

21 Special insertions

LaTeX provides commands for inserting characters that have a special meaning do not correspond to simple characters you can type.

21.1 Reserved characters

LaTeX sets aside the following characters for special purposes (for example, the percent sign % is for comments) so they are called *reserved characters* or *special characters*.

```
# $ % & { } _ ~ ^ \
```

If you want a reserved character to be printed as itself, in the text body font, for all but the final three characters in that list simply put a backslash \ in front of the character. Thus, `\$1.23` will produce `$1.23` in your output.

As to the last three characters, to get a tilde in the text body font use `\~{}` (omitting the curly braces would result in the next character receiving a tilde accent). Similarly, to get a get a text body font circumflex use `\^{}`. A text body font backslash results from `\textbackslash{}`.

To produce the reserved characters in a typewriter font use `\verb!!`, as below.

```
\begin{center}
  \# \$ \% \& \{ \} \_ \~{} \^{} \textbackslash \\
  \verb!# $ % & { } _ ~ ^ \!
\end{center}
```

In that example the double backslash \\ is only there to split the lines.

21.2 Upper and lower case

Synopsis:

```
\uppercase{text}
\lowercase{text}
\MakeUppercase{text}
\MakeLowercase{text}
```

Change the case of characters. The TeX primitives commands `\uppercase` and `\lowercase` only work for American characters. The LaTeX commands `\MakeUppercase` and `\MakeLowercase` commands also change characters accessed by commands such as `\ae` or `\aa`. The commands `\MakeUppercase` and `\MakeLowercase` are robust but they have moving arguments (see Section 12.9 [\protect], page 78).

These commands do not change the case of letters used in the name of a command within *text*. But they do change the case of every other latin character inside the argument *text*. Thus, `\MakeUppercase{Let $y=f(x)$}` produces "LET Y=F(X)". Another example is that the name of an environment will be changed, so that `\MakeUppercase{\begin{tabular} ... \end{tabular}` will produce an error because the first half is changed to `\begin{TABULAR}`.

LaTeX uses the same fixed table for changing case throughout a document, The table used is designed for the font encoding T1; this works well with the standard TeX fonts for all Latin alphabets but will cause problems when using other alphabets.

To change the case of text that results from a command inside *text* you need to do expansion. Here the `\Schoolname` produces "COLLEGE OF MATHEMATICS".

```
\newcommand{\schoolname}{College of Mathematics}
\newcommand{\Schoolname}{\expandafter\MakeUppercase\expandafter{\schoolname}}
```

To uppercase only the first letter of words use the package `mfirstuc`.

21.3 Symbols by font position

You can access any character of the current font using its number with the `\symbol` command. For example, the visible space character used in the `\verb*` command has the code decimal 32, so it can be typed as `\symbol{32}`.

You can also specify numbers in octal (base 8) by using a ' prefix, or hexadecimal (base 16) with a " prefix, so the previous example could also be written as `\symbol{'40}` or `\symbol{"20}`.

21.4 Text symbols

LaTeX provides commands to generate a number of non-letter symbols in running text. Some of these, especially the more obscure ones, are not available in OT1; you may need to load the `textcomp` package.

`\copyright`
`\textcopyright`
> The copyright symbol, ©.

`\dag`   The dagger symbol (in text).

`\ddag`   The double dagger symbol (in text).

`\LaTeX`   The LaTeX logo.

`\LaTeXe`   The LaTeX2e logo.

`\guillemotleft` («)
`\guillemotright` (»)
`\guilsinglleft` (‹)
`\guilsinglright` (›)
> Double and single angle quotation marks, commonly used in French: «, », ‹, ›.

`\ldots`
`\dots`
`\textellipsis`
> An ellipsis (three dots at the baseline): '...'. `\ldots` and `\dots` also work in math mode.

`\lq`   Left (opening) quote: '.

`\P`
`\textparagraph`
> Paragraph sign (pilcrow): ¶.

`\pounds`
`\textsterling`
> English pounds sterling: £.

`\quotedblbase` („)
`\quotesinglbase` (‚)

> Double and single quotation marks on the baseline: „ and ‚.

`\rq`   Right (closing) quote: '.

`\S`   `\itemx \textsection` Section sign: §.

`\TeX`   The TeX logo.

`\textasciicircum`

> ASCII circumflex: ˆ.

`\textasciitilde`

> ASCII tilde: ˜.

`\textasteriskcentered`

> Centered asterisk: *.

`\textbackslash`

> Backslash: \.

`\textbar`   Vertical bar: |.

`\textbardbl`

> Double vertical bar.

`\textbigcircle`

> Big circle symbol.

`\textbraceleft`

> Left brace: {.

`\textbraceright`

> Right brace: }.

`\textbullet`

> Bullet: •.

`\textcircled{letter}`

> *letter* in a circle, as in ®.

`\textcompwordmark`
`\textcapitalcompwordmark`
`\textascendercompwordmark`

> Composite word mark (invisible). The `\textcapital...` form has the cap height of the font, while the `\textascender...` form has the ascender height.

`\textdagger`

> Dagger: †.

`\textdaggerdbl`

> Double dagger: ‡.

`\textdollar` (or `\$`)

> Dollar sign: $.

`\textemdash` (or `---`)
>	Em-dash: — (for punctuation).

`\textendash` (or `--`)
>	En-dash: – (for ranges).

`\texteuro`
>	The Euro symbol: €.

`\textexclamdown` (or `!`)
>	Upside down exclamation point: ¡.

`\textgreater`
>	Greater than: >.

`\textless`
>	Less than: <.

`\textleftarrow`
>	Left arrow.

`\textordfeminine`
`\textordmasculine`
>	Feminine and masculine ordinal symbols: ª, º.

`\textperiodcentered`
>	Centered period: ·.

`\textquestiondown` (or `?`)
>	Upside down question mark: ¿.

`\textquotedblleft` (or ``)
>	Double left quote: ".

`\textquotedblright` (or `''`)
>	Double right quote: ".

`\textquoteleft` (or `)
>	Single left quote: '.

`\textquoteright` (or `'`)
>	Single right quote: '.

`\textquotesingle`
>	Straight single quote. (From TS1 encoding.)

`\textquotestraightbase`
`\textquotestraightdblbase`
>	Single and double straight quotes on the baseline.

`\textregistered`
>	Registered symbol: ®.

`\textrightarrow`
>	Right arrow.

`\textthreequartersemdash`
>	"Three-quarters" em-dash, between en-dash and em-dash.

`\texttrademark`
>   Trademark symbol: TM.

`\texttwelveudash`
>   "Two-thirds" em-dash, between en-dash and em-dash.

`\textunderscore`
>   Underscore: _.

`\textvisiblespace`
>   Visible space symbol.

21.5 Accents

LaTeX has wide support for many of the world's scripts and languages, through the `babel` package and related support. This section does not attempt to cover all that support. It merely lists the core LaTeX commands for creating accented characters.

The `\capital...` commands produce alternative forms for use with capital letters. These are not available with OT1.

`\"`
`\capitaldieresis`
>   Produces an umlaut (dieresis), as in ö.

`\'`
`\capitalacute`
>   Produces an acute accent, as in ó. In the **tabbing** environment, pushes current column to the right of the previous column (see Section 8.21 [tabbing], page 54).

`\.`   Produces a dot accent over the following, as in ȯ.

`\=`
`\capitalmacron`
>   Produces a macron (overbar) accent over the following, as in ō.

`\^`
`\capitalcircumflex`
>   Produces a circumflex (hat) accent over the following, as in ô.

`\`` `
`\capitalgrave`
>   Produces a grave accent over the following, as in ò. In the **tabbing** environment, move following text to the right margin (see Section 8.21 [tabbing], page 54).

`\~`
`\capitaltilde`
>   Produces a tilde accent over the following, as in ñ.

`\b`   Produces a bar accent under the following, as in o̲. See also `\underbar` hereinafter.

`\c`
`\capitalcedilla`
>   Produces a cedilla accent under the following, as in ç.

`\d`
`\capitaldotaccent`

> Produces a dot accent under the following, as in ọ.

`\H`
`\capitalhungarumlaut`

> Produces a long Hungarian umlaut accent over the following, as in ő.

`\i`   Produces a dotless i, as in 'ı'.

`\j`   Produces a dotless j, as in 'ȷ'.

`\k`
`\capitalogonek`

> Produces a letter with ogonek, as in 'ǫ'. Not available in the OT1 encoding.

`\r`
`\capitalring`

> Produces a ring accent, as in 'å̊'.

`\t`
`\capitaltie`
`\newtie`
`\capitalnewtie`

> Produces a tie-after accent, as in 'o͡o'. The `\newtie` form is centered in its box.

`\u`
`\capitalbreve`

> Produces a breve accent, as in 'ŏ'.

`\underbar`

> Not exactly an accent, this produces a bar under the argument text. The argument is always processed in horizontal mode. The bar is always a fixed position under the baseline, thus crossing through descenders. See also `\underline` in Section 16.6 [Math miscellany], page 100. See also `\b` above.

`\v`
`\capitalcaron`

> Produces a háček (check, caron) accent, as in 'ǒ'.

21.6 Additional Latin letters

Here are the basic LaTeX commands for inserting letters (beyond A–Z) extending the Latin alphabet, used primarily in languages other than English.

`\aa`
`\AA`   å and Å.

`\ae`
`\AE`   æ and Æ.

`\dh`
`\DH`   Icelandic letter eth: ð and Ð. Not available with OT1 encoding, you need the `fontenc` package to select an alternate font encoding, such as T1.

\dj \DJ	Crossed d and D, a.k.a. capital and small letter d with stroke. Not available with OT1 encoding, you need the `fontenc` package to select an alternate font encoding, such as T1.
\ij \IJ	ij and IJ (except somewhat closer together than appears here).
\l \L	ł and Ł.
\ng \NG	Lappish letter eng, also used in phonetics.
\o \O	ø and Ø.
\oe \OE	œ and Œ.
\ss \SS	ß and SS.
\th \TH	Icelandic letter thorn: þ and Þ. Not available with OT1 encoding, you need the `fontenc` package to select an alternate font encoding, such as T1.

21.7 \rule

Synopsis:

> \rule[*raise*]{*width*}{*thickness*}

The \rule command produces *rules*, that is, lines or rectangles. The arguments are:

raise   How high to raise the rule (optional).

width   The length of the rule (mandatory).

thickness   The thickness of the rule (mandatory).

21.8 \today

The \today command produces today's date, in the format '*month dd, yyyy*'; for example, 'July 4, 1976'. It uses the predefined counters \day, \month, and \year (see Section 13.8 [\day \month \year], page 82) to do this. It is not updated as the program runs.

Multilingual packages like `babel` or classes like `lettre`, among others, will localize \today. For example, the following will output '4 juillet 1976':

> \year=1976 \month=7 \day=4
> \documentclass{minimal}
> \usepackage[french]{babel}
> \begin{document}
> \today
> \end{document}

The `datetime` package, among others, can produce a wide variety of other date formats.

22 Splitting the input

A large document requires a lot of input. Rather than putting the whole input in a single large file, it's more efficient to split it into several smaller ones. Regardless of how many separate files you use, there is one that is the *root file*; it is the one whose name you type when you run LaTeX.

See Section 8.11 [filecontents], page 45, for an environment that allows bundling an external file to be created with the main document.

22.1 \include

Synopsis:

    \include{*file*}

If no \includeonly command is present, the \include command executes \clearpage to start a new page (see Section 10.2 [\clearpage], page 67), then reads *file*, then does another \clearpage.

Given an \includeonly command, the \include actions are only run if *file* is listed as an argument to \includeonly. See Section 22.2 [\includeonly], page 121.

The \include command may not appear in the preamble or in a file read by another \include command.

22.2 \includeonly

Synopsis:

    \includeonly{*file1*,*file2*,...}

The \includeonly command controls which files will be read by subsequent \include commands. The list of filenames is comma-separated. Each element *file1*, *file2*, ... must exactly match a filename specified in a \include command for the selection to be effective.

This command can only appear in the preamble.

22.3 \input

Synopsis:

    \input{*file*}

The \input command causes the specified *file* to be read and processed, as if its contents had been inserted in the current file at that point.

If *file* does not end in '.tex' (e.g., 'foo' or 'foo.bar'), it is first tried with that extension ('foo.tex' or 'foo.bar.tex'). If that is not found, the original *file* is tried ('foo' or 'foo.bar').

23 Front/back matter

23.1 Tables of contents

A table of contents is produced with the `\tableofcontents` command. You put the command right where you want the table of contents to go; LATEX does the rest for you. A previous run must have generated a `.toc` file.

The `\tableofcontents` command produces a heading, but it does not automatically start a new page. If you want a new page after the table of contents, write a `\newpage` command after the `\tableofcontents` command.

The analogous commands `\listoffigures` and `\listoftables` produce a list of figures and a list of tables (from `.lof` and `.lot` files), respectively. Everything works exactly the same as for the table of contents.

The command `\nofiles` overrides these commands, and *prevents* any of these lists from being generated.

23.1.1 \addcontentsline

Synopsis:

    \addcontentsline{ext}{unit}{text}

The `\addcontentsline` command adds an entry to the specified list or table where:

ext   The filename extension of the file on which information is to be written, typically one of: `toc` (table of contents), `lof` (list of figures), or `lot` (list of tables).

unit   The name of the sectional unit being added, typically one of the following, matching the value of the *ext* argument:

         `toc`   The name of the sectional unit: `part`, `chapter`, `section`, `subsection`, `subsubsection`.

         `lof`   For the list of figures: `figure`.

         `lot`   For the list of tables: `table`.

text   The text of the entry.

What is written to the `.ext` file is the command `\contentsline{unit}{text}{num}`, where `num` is the current value of counter `unit`.

23.1.2 \addtocontents

The `\addtocontents{ext}{text}` command adds text (or formatting commands) directly to the `.ext` file that generates the table of contents or lists of figures or tables.

ext   The extension of the file on which information is to be written, typically one of: `toc` (table of contents), `lof` (list of figures), or `lot` (list of tables).

text   The text to be written.

23.2 Glossaries

The command `\makeglossary` enables creating glossaries.

The command `\glossary{text}` writes a glossary entry for *text* to an auxiliary file with the `.glo` extension.

Specifically, what gets written is the command `\glossaryentry{text}{pageno}`, where *pageno* is the current `\thepage` value.

The `glossary` package on CTAN provides support for fancier glossaries.

23.3 Indexes

The command `\makeindex` enables creating indexes. Put this in the preamble.

The command `\index{text}` writes an index entry for *text* to an auxiliary file named with the `.idx` extension.

Specifically, what gets written is the command `\indexentry{text}{pageno}`, where *pageno* is the current `\thepage` value.

To generate a index entry for 'bar' that says 'See foo', use a vertical bar: `\index{bar|see{foo}}`. Use `seealso` instead of `see` to make a 'See also' entry.

The text 'See' is defined by the macro `\seename`, and 'See also' by the macro `\alsoname`. These can be redefined for other languages.

The generated `.idx` file is then sorted with an external command, usually either `makeindex` (`http://mirror.ctan.org/indexing/makeindex`) or (the multi-lingual) `xindy` (`http://xindy.sourceforge.net`). This results in a `.ind` file, which can then be read to typeset the index.

The index is usually generated with the `\printindex` command. This is defined in the `makeidx` package, so `\usepackage{makeidx}` needs to be in the preamble.

The rubber length `\indexspace` is inserted before each new letter in the printed index; its default value is '`10pt plus5pt minus3pt`'.

The `showidx` package causes each index entries to be shown in the margin on the page where the entry appears. This can help in preparing the index.

The `multind` package supports multiple indexes. See also the TeX FAQ entry on this topic, `http://www.tex.ac.uk/cgi-bin/texfaq2html?label=multind`.

24 Letters

Synopsis:

```
\documentclass{letter}
\address{sender address}
\signature{sender name}
\begin{document}
\begin{letter}{recipient address}
\opening{salutation}
  letter body
\closing{closing text}
\end{letter}
... more letters ...
\end{document}
```

Produce one or more letters.

Each letter is in a separate `letter` environment, whose argument *recipient address* often contains multiple lines separated with a double backslash (\\). For example, you might have:

```
\begin{letter}{Mr. Joe Smith \\
    2345 Princess St. \\
    Edinburgh, EH1 1AA}
  ...
\end{letter}
```

The start of the `letter` environment resets the page number to 1, and the footnote number to 1 also.

The *sender address* and *sender name* are common to all of the letters, whether there is one or more, so these are best put in the preamble. As with the recipient address, often *sender address* contains multiple lines separated by a double backslash (\\). LaTeX will put the *sender name* under the closing, after a vertical space for the traditional hand-written signature; it also can contain multiple lines.

Each `letter` environment body begins with a required `\opening` command such as `\opening{Dear Madam or Sir:}`. The *letter body* text is ordinary LaTeX so it can contain everything from enumerated lists to displayed math, except that commands such as `\chapter` that make no sense in a letter are turned off. Each `letter` environment body typically ends with a `\closing` command such as `\closing{Yours,}`.

Additional material may come after the `\closing`. You can say who is receiving a copy of the letter with a command like `\cc{the Boss \\ the Boss's Boss}`. There's a similar `\encl` command for a list of enclosures. And, you can add a postscript with `\ps`.

LaTeX's default is to indent the signature and the `\closing` above it by a length of `\longindentation`. By default this is `0.5\textwidth`. To make them flush left, put `\setlength{\longindentation}{0em}` in your preamble.

To set a fixed date use something like `\renewcommand{\today}{2015-Oct-12}`. If put in your preamble then it will apply to all the letters.

This example shows only one `letter` environment. The three lines marked as optional are typically omitted.

```
\documentclass{letter}
\address{Sender's street \\ Sender's town}
\signature{Sender's name \\ Sender's title}
% optional: \location{Mailbox 13}
% optional: \telephone{(102) 555-0101}
\begin{document}
\begin{letter}{Recipient's name \\ Recipient's address}
\opening{Sir:}
% optional: \thispagestyle{firstpage}
I am not interested in entering a business arrangement with you.
\closing{Your most humble, etc.,}
\end{letter}
\end{document}
```

These commands are used with the `letter` class.

24.1 \address

Synopsis:

```
\address{senders address}
```

Specifies the return address as it appears on the letter and on the envelope. Separate multiple lines in *senders address* with a double backslash \\.

Because it can apply to multiple letters this declaration is often put in the preamble. However, it can go anywhere, including inside an individual `letter` environment.

This command is optional: without the `\address` declaration the letter is formatted with some blank space on top, for copying onto pre-printed letterhead paper. (See Chapter 2 [Overview], page 3, for details on your local implementation.) With the `\address` declaration, it is formatted as a personal letter.

Here is an example.

```
\address{Stephen Maturin \\
         The Grapes of the Savoy}
```

24.2 \cc

Synopsis:

```
\cc{first name \\
    ... }
```

Produce a list of names to which copies of the letter were sent. This command is optional. If it appears then typically it comes after `\closing`. Separate multiple lines with a double backslash \\, as in:

```
\cc{President \\
    Vice President}
```

24.3 \closing

Synopsis:

> \closing{*text*}

Usually at the end of a letter, above the handwritten signature, there is a \closing (although this command is optional). For example,

> \closing{Regards,}

24.4 \encl

Synopsis:

> \encl{*first enclosed object* \\
>   ... }

Produce a list of things included with the letter. This command is optional; when it is used, it typically is put after \closing. Separate multiple lines with a double backslash \\.

> \encl{License \\
>   Passport }

24.5 \location

Synopsis:

> \location{*text*}

The *text* appears centered at the bottom of the each page. It only appears if the page style is firstpage.

24.6 \makelabels

Synopsis:

> \makelabels

Create a sheet of address labels from the recipient addresses, one for each letter. This sheet will be output before the letters, with the idea that you can copy it to a sheet of peel-off labels. This command goes in the preamble.

Customize the labels by redefining the commands \startlabels, \mlabel, and \returnaddress in the preamble. The command \startlabels sets the width, height, number of columns, etc., of the page onto which the labels are printed. The command \mlabel{*sender address*}{*recipient address*} produces the two labels (or one, if you choose to ignore the *sender address*). The *sender address* is the value returned by the macro \returnaddress while *recipient address* is the value passed in the argument to the letter environment. By default \mlabel ignores the first argument, the *sender address*.

24.7 \name

Synopsis:

> \name{*name*}

Sender's name, used for printing on the envelope together with the return address.

24.8 \opening

Synopsis:

    \opening{text}

This command is required. It starts a letter, following the \begin{letter}{...}. The mandatory argument *text* is the text that starts your letter. For instance:

    \opening{Dear John:}

24.9 \ps

Synopsis:

    \ps{text}

Add a postscript. This command is optional and usually is used after \closing.

    \ps{P.S. After you have read this letter, burn it. Or eat it.}

24.10 \signature

Synopsis:

    \signature{first line \\
                ... }

The sender's name. This command is optional, although its inclusion is usual.

The argument text appears at the end of the letter, after the closing and after a vertical space for the traditional hand-written signature. Separate multiple lines with a double backslash \\. For example:

    \signature{J Fred Muggs \\
                White House}

LaTeX's default for the vertical space from the \closing text down to the \signature text is 6\medskipamount, which is six times 0.7 em.

This command is usually in the preamble, to apply to all the letters in the document. To have it apply to one letter only, put it inside a letter environment and before the \closing.

You can include a graphic in the signature, for instance with \signature{\vspace{-6\medskipamount}\in⟨ My name} (this requires writing \usepackage{graphicx} in the preamble).

24.11 \telephone

Synopsis:

    \telephone{number}

The sender's telephone number. This is typically in the preamble, where it applies to all letters. This only appears if the firstpage pagestyle is selected. If so, it appears on the lower right of the page.

25 Terminal input/output

25.1 \typein[*cmd*]{*msg*}

Synopsis:

> \typein[*cmd*]{*msg*}

\typein prints *msg* on the terminal and causes LaTeX to stop and wait for you to type a line of input, ending with return. If the optional *cmd* argument is omitted, the typed input is processed as if it had been included in the input file in place of the \typein command. If the *cmd* argument is present, it must be a command name. This command name is then defined or redefined to be the typed input.

25.2 \typeout{*msg*}

Synopsis:

> \typeout{*msg*}

Prints msg on the terminal and in the log file. Commands in msg that are defined with \newcommand or \renewcommand (among others) are replaced by their definitions before being printed.

LaTeX's usual rules for treating multiple spaces as a single space and ignoring spaces after a command name apply to msg. A \space command in msg causes a single space to be printed, independent of surrounding spaces. A ^^J in msg prints a newline.

26 Command line

The input file specification indicates the file to be formatted; TeX uses `.tex` as a default file extension. If you omit the input file entirely, TeX accepts input from the terminal. You can also specify arbitrary LaTeX input by starting with a backslash. For example, this processes `foo.tex` without pausing after every error:

```
latex '\nonstopmode\input foo.tex'
```

With many, but not all, implementations, command-line options can also be specified in the usual Unix way, starting with '-' or '--'. For a list of those options, try '`latex --help`'.

If LaTeX stops in the middle of the document and gives you a '`*`' prompt, it is waiting for input. You can type `\stop` (and return) and it will prematurely end the document.

See Section 2.3 [TeX engines], page 4, for other system commands invoking LaTeX.

Appendix A Document templates

Although not reference material, perhaps these document templates will be useful. Additional template resources are listed at `http://tug.org/interest.html#latextemplates`.

A.1 beamer template

The `beamer` class creates presentation slides. It has a vast array of features, but here is a basic template:

```
\documentclass{beamer}

\title{Beamer Class template}
\author{Alex Author}
\date{July 31, 2007}

\begin{document}

\maketitle

% without [fragile], any {verbatim} code gets mysterious errors.
\begin{frame}[fragile]
 \frametitle{First Slide}

\begin{verbatim}
  This is \verbatim!
\end{verbatim}

\end{frame}

\end{document}
```

One web resource for this: `http://robjhyndman.com/hyndsight/beamer/`.

A.2 book template

```
\documentclass{book}
\title{Book Class Template}
\author{Alex Author}

\begin{document}
\maketitle

\chapter{First}
Some text.

\chapter{Second}
Some other text.
```

```
\section{A subtopic}
The end.
\end{document}
```

A.3 tugboat template

TUGboat is the journal of the TeX Users Group, http://tug.org/TUGboat.

```
\documentclass{ltugboat}

\usepackage{graphicx}
\usepackage{ifpdf}
\ifpdf
\usepackage[breaklinks,hidelinks]{hyperref}
\else
\usepackage{url}
\fi

%%% Start of metadata %%%

\title{Example \TUB\ article}

% repeat info for each author.
\author{First Last}
\address{Street Address \\ Town, Postal \\ Country}
\netaddress{user (at) example dot org}
\personalURL{http://example.org/~user/}

%%% End of metadata %%%

\begin{document}

\maketitle

\begin{abstract}
This is an example article for \TUB{}.
Please write an abstract.
\end{abstract}

\section{Introduction}

This is an example article for \TUB, linked from
\url{http://tug.org/TUGboat/location.html}.

We recommend the \texttt{graphicx} package for image inclusions, and the
\texttt{hyperref} package if active urls are desired (in the \acro{PDF}
output).  Nowadays \TUB\ is produced using \acro{PDF} files exclusively.
```

```
The \texttt{ltugboat} class provides these abbreviations (and many more):
% verbatim blocks are often better in \small
\begin{verbatim}[\small]
\AllTeX \AMS \AmS \AmSLaTeX \AmSTeX \aw \AW
\BibTeX \CTAN \DTD \HTML
\ISBN \ISSN \LaTeXe
\mf \MFB
\plain \POBox \PS
\SGML \TANGLE \TB \TP
\TUB \TUG \tug
\UNIX \XeT \WEB \WEAVE

\, \bull \Dash \dash \hyph

\acro{FRED} -> {\small[er] fred}  % please use!
\cs{fred}   -> \fred
\meta{fred} -> <fred>
\nth{n}     -> 1st, 2nd, ...
\sfrac{3/4} -> 3/4
\booktitle{Book of Fred}
\end{verbatim}

For references to other \TUB\ issue, please use the format
\textsl{volno:issno}, e.g., ''\TUB\ 32:1'' for our \nth{100} issue.

This file is just a template.  The \TUB\ style documentation is the
\texttt{ltubguid} document at \url{http://ctan.org/pkg/tugboat}.  (For
\CTAN\ references, where sensible we recommend that form of url, using
\texttt{/pkg/}; or, if you need to refer to a specific file location,
\texttt{http://mirror.ctan.org/\textsl{path}}.)

Email \verb|tugboat@tug.org| if problems or questions.

\bibliographystyle{plain}  % we recommend the plain bibliography style
\nocite{book-minimal}      % just making the bibliography non-empty
\bibliography{xampl}       % xampl.bib comes with BibTeX

\makesignature
\end{document}
```

Concept Index

Command Index